BIG

QUESTIONS
IN
CREATIVITY

2015

D1428382

BIG
QUESTIONS
IN
CREATIVITY
2015

EDITED BY
MARY KAY CULPEPPER
& CYNTHIA BURNETT

A COLLECTION OF FIRST WORKS, VOLUME 3

ICSC Press
International Center for Studies in Creativity
Buffalo State, State University of New York
Buffalo, NY, U.S.A.

INTERNATIONAL CENTER *for* STUDIES *in* CREATIVITY

BUFFALO STATE · The State University of New York

ICSC Press
International Center for Studies in Creativity
Buffalo State, The State University of New York
1300 Elmwood Avenue
Buffalo, NY 14222, USA
icscpress.com

© 2015 by ICSC Press

ISBN: 978-0-9849795-4-7 (print edition)

Library of Congress Control Number: 2015907979

Simultaneously published in multiple formats, both print and electronic.
For alternative versions and to discover other titles, visit icscpress.com.

Book Design and Graphics: Kevin D. Opp

To the memory of creativity pioneer E. Paul Torrance
(1915-2003), born 100 years ago,
who asked so many of the best questions, and
continues to inspire creativity scholars to ask their own.

Contents

Introduction

S tudying creativity will change you," one editor of this book advised the other a few years ago. "I've seen it happen time and again: with this study, people have a broader sense of what is possible in their lives. They see a bigger world, and they want to be a part of it."

Of course, she was right. In the ensuing time, we both have witnessed the field's transformative sweep propel ourselves, our colleagues, and our students to imagine a different world—and set about making it happen. Without exception, that is the force that galvanizes the authors of this collection, compelling them to ask questions now that will drive them as they undertake careers and lives shaped by the answers.

The New Edition

Big Questions in Creativity 2015 is the third installment in what promises to be a long-running title featuring first papers in creativity. The nationwide call for papers made last year requested works that ask and answer an open question in the field. Dozens of submissions from promising scholars around the world showed a range of ideas that exemplify the remarkable breadth of what creativity is considered to be now, and what it may well be in the future.

The independently-developed essays selected for this anthology are an initial foray for their authors in the academic proclamation of their creative convictions. As suits the brief, the works strike a reflexive—rather than pedagogic—tone. As it happens, that suits the real-world experience of the authors, too: they are professional facilitators, artists, educators, and change leaders. They work to engender creativity in others. To a person, they began studying creativity because it is essential to what they do.

Accordingly, their papers ask and reply to questions that shed light on the ways that people and their social structures encourage and manage creativity. While their essays address multiple topics, three key themes emerged—Personal Creativity, Organizational Creativity, and Systems of Creativity—and they form the sections of this book.

Personal Creativity

If the creative experience has the potential to effect lasting change, examining its influence on individuals could identify how its power can be harnessed to help people live more fully. A moving moment at his daughter's school play convinced Geoff Zoeckler to consider the effect of empathy—of taking the wants, needs, and hopes of another—into the realm of creative problem solving.

In her study of problem solving, Jane Harvey noticed that the basic human trait of curiosity underscores the impulse to create. The research she analyzed led her to an intriguing insight: wondering about something is the precursor to considering it creatively.

After being fueled by curiosity, a person's creative orientation is fed by play, assert Juliana Sánchez-Trujillo and Erica Swiatek. While the role of play in childhood is well explored, they extended the scope of their inquiry to adult learners. Not only do they suggest that play is beneficial for enhancing creativity in the non-traditional student, they offer strategies for incorporating it in the classroom.

Organizational Creativity

One impetus for including creativity in a curriculum is that companies demand it of potential employees. Yet channeling creative thought and action in corporations is often at odds with the demands of efficient production and the economic realities of the bottom line. W. Clayton Bunyard explores a prominent approach for workplace efficiency—continuous improvement—and identifies ways it might more effectively allow for creativity and innovation.

The advantages of creative thinking go beyond product and process innovation. David Eyman's own practice as a creativity consultant informed his essay on the hidden yet undeniably valuable benefits of group creativity techniques such as brainstorming: shared experience, common vision, and an enhanced understanding of larger goals.

Those effects find an echo in Troy Schubert's paper. His first-person account of advocating for positive change in his workplace lays bare the uncertainties inherent in the creative process, and clarifies why tolerating ambiguity is essential; in the end, promoting personal and organizational faith in creativity can affect lives and futures.

Systems of Creativity

The interchange between the individual and the larger world—that is, the societies and cultures we all take part in—informs the systems approach to considering creativity, and two articles take the systems of nature as their starting point. Jennifer A. Quarrie contemplates biomimetics as means of enhancing creativity, while Kathryn P. Haydon finds the prairie ecosystem a fruitful metaphor for the education system. Both authors see in nature a system of systems that generates inspiration for solving human problems.

The perspective that arises from such solutions could foster international understanding. Gaia Grant examines contrasting conceptions of creativity from around the world and identifies how they emerge from sociocultural systems.

Ultimately, different systems and problems require different approaches, contends Courtney Zwart. Her examination of design thinking—itself a systems approach—finds that it is ideal for some problems, while Creative Problem Solving is better for others.

Conclusion

These questions have important implications not just for the questioners, but for all of us. By identifying what could make the world a kinder, more enlightened, more equitable place, the authors in this volume make a persuasive case for creativity in the service for change.

Creativity—both as a field of study and as a phenomenon of experience—demands novelty, vision, and a sense of wonder. Because change is in the essence of creativity, we can all demand of it new ways of seeing and being in the world.

Mary Kay Culpepper
London, England

Cynthia Burnett
Buffalo, NY

PERSONAL
CREATIVITY

What Is the Return On Empathy? Can it Be Used as a Creative Problem Solving Tool?

Geoff G. Zoeckler
International Center for Studies in Creativity
SUNY Buffalo State

Abstract

Empathy has developed into a topic of wide discussion and focused research. While the most common definition is to put oneself into the shoes of another, empathy goes beyond just perspective taking. The two forms of empathy, contagious and cognitive, both require the perceiver to feel what the target is feeling, thereby creating a visceral experience and a compulsion to act. Empathy leads to a desire for action and can, therefore, be viewed as part of a creative problem solving process. It can change lives and create transformation for both the perceiver and the target. To better understand the possible benefits of choosing empathy, it is important to investigate research from neuroscience and psychology while linking the findings to applied examples in a variety of settings. This paper addresses what empathy is, why we do or don't choose it, how it works, and how it can be used to solve problems.

What Is the Return On Empathy? Can it Be Used as a Creative Problem Solving Tool?

Earlier this year, I attended a musical performance put on by my daughter's second grade class. On the stage that evening, an unplanned story played out that led me to question the purpose and power of empathy.

My oldest daughter, Lily, had been practicing her part in the show for more than two months. As we got ready to leave for the performance, I could feel Lily's excitement and nervousness. We arrived at the auditorium, released Lily into the chaos, and found our seats.

The curtains rose, the musical began, and everything seemed like a typical show. The 7- and 8-year-olds were singing and dancing, except for one. On the far right side of the stage, there was a student with special needs named Sammy.

It was clear that Sammy was anxious. He began to stomp his feet and flail his arms. As that began, a visible separation formed between Sammy and the rest of the students. As I watched from the audience, a wave of sadness swept over me. I started to imagine what Sammy's life must be like at school, constantly feeling as if on the other side of a wall, and unable to feel part of the group. As Sammy continued to stomp, I felt certain that someone was going to need to intervene and possibly take him off stage. Then something interesting happened: the girl standing next to Sammy reached out and held his hand.

In that one small act, the wall between Sammy and the rest of his classmates completely dissolved. A second-grade world of cooties, icky boys, peer pressure, and embarrassment was washed away for a moment, and the simple act of holding another's hand changed the course of the evening. Not just for Sammy (who calmed down and stayed on stage for the entire performance), but for the entire audience.

The act was a form of empathy for all to see. While I had been sitting in my chair feeling sadness for Sammy, the girl next to him felt his anxiety and then acted upon it. Her simple gesture was more expansive than it seemed; in that venue, it was as if she extended a hand to us all.

Her small act of empathy that evening was a reminder that we are all very nearly the same. There's a power in understanding that we are 99.9% genetically identical (Zhivotovsky, Rosenberg, & Feldman, 2003), and that we all experience a common set of emotions (Plutchik, 2001). This commonality drives to a similar set of basic human needs that we can all understand.

Lily was the girl who reached out to hold Sammy's hand. Because she is my daughter, I pursued a deeper path of questioning. What allowed her to break through and hold his hand? Why did she do it? Why doesn't everyone always act that way? Can empathic behavior be taught? Can empathy be used to solve problems? Is it related to creativity?

To better understand the construct of empathy, my key question became, "What is the return on empathy?" This paper, in an attempt to answer it, explores what empathy is, why we have it, when we do and don't use it, and how we might choose an empathic approach.

What Is Empathy?

Empathy is most often described as putting oneself in the shoes of another. It is particularly useful when seeking to understand emotional information, and it includes two individuals. The perceiver, or self, is the individual focusing on the emotional state of the other. The target, or other, is the individual who is being focused on. Therefore, another way to describe empathy would be: a perceiver striving to understand the emotional context and needs of the target. This is a reasonable summary, but it's only part of the definition. In itself, it risks falling short into an experience of sympathy. To paint the full picture, empathy can be understood as having at least two distinctly different forms: contagious and cognitive. (A third form, empathic motivation (Zaki & Ochsner, 2012), is more closely related to sympathy. As it does not often result in action on the part of the perceiver, it is beyond the scope of this paper.)

Contagious Empathy

Contagious empathy, also referred to as emotional contagion (Zaki & Ochsner, 2012), is a natural process that occurs without conscious effort. It adjusts the perceiver's mental and emotional state to be closer to that of the target, which often results in action. This form of empathy is demonstrated in humans at birth. Consider babies in a hospital nursery: when one baby starts to cry, the babies that are near often begin to cry (Rifkin, 2009). Or consider the action of a bystander who, in a moment of unconscious heroism, rushes into traffic to push another out of the way of an oncoming car. In a split second, the emotional context and needs of another are understood and acted upon.

It can be argued that contagious empathy is inherent in humans because of our biological makeup. In the past decade, neuroscientists have begun to study this side of empathy with a focus on brain activity (e.g., Bernhardt & Singer, 2012; Blakeslee, 2006; Decety, 2010; Decety, Chen, Harenski, & Kiehl, 2013; Zaki & Ochsner, 2012). Many of their findings examine the brain's neurons. Neurons do many things, but certain neurons seem to mimic the behavior or emotional experience of another person. These mirror neurons behave as if the observer is acting even though he or she is passive. Mirror neurons appear to better allow the perceiver to identify emotions and relate to the target. Earlier studies have shown there are entire regions of the brain that cannot tell the difference between the response of self and other, supporting the idea that humans are wired for empathy (Iacoboni, 2009). "Mirror neurons show the deepest way we relate to and understand each other: they demonstrate how we are wired for empathy, which should inspire us to shape our society and make it a better place to live" (Iacoboni, 2009, pp. 267-268). Decety and Jackson (2004) put it more directly: "The basic building blocks are hardwired in the brain and await development through interaction with others" (p. 71).

Cognitive Empathy

Cognitive empathy, also referred to as perspective taking, is a conscious decision to understand and take on the emotional needs of another. This is the most commonly discussed form of empathy in topics such as design thinking and user-centered design (Liedtka & Ogilvie, 2011). Examples of shared empathy often include deep ethnographic research studies (research conducted while spending hours or days personally involved in the life of another) followed by adjusting a perceiver's situation to be more like that of the target. This choice to "put yourself in the shoes of another" is a conscious one, and it requires substantially more energy than contagious empathy.

Both cognitive and contagious empathy go beyond the observation of another's emotions or experiences. They also extend to a visceral experience for the affected perceiver, and that evokes motivation to help others (Wieseke, Geigenmuller, & Kraus, 2012). In other words, the perceiver takes on another's emotions. This compels one to act on the behalf of another.

To arrive at a functional definition of empathy, then, we need to combine both forms of empathy into one definition. To do so, I offer the following equation:

$$Head + Heart = Gut$$

Head is in reference to what you observe. *Heart* is in reference to what is happening to you emotionally. *Gut* is in reference to a desire to act based on what you observed and felt. Or, as stated in the training materials of SEEK Company (2014), an empathy-based innovation consultancy, "Empathy is allowing what is coming into your head to affect your heart, thereby compelling you to act upon the needs of another."

Why We Choose Empathy–and Why We Do Not

One explanation for empathic behavior is that empathy is required for the survival of our species (Greene, 2012). Millennia ago, survival depended on group effort. The many were stronger than the one, and what was best for the group became best for the individual. This made empathy toward another mutually beneficial. Through a combination of contagious and cognitive empathy, an individual could understand the needs of others and then work to solve problems on behalf of the group as a whole.

Another perspective is that empathy has been developed as a way to advance the quest for a Utopian society. Throughout history, technological advances in communication, coupled with intrinsic empathic nature, have led to collaboration first within families, then within religious groups, and now into areas of national identity (Rifkin, 2009). It could be possible that our human drive for empathy will continue to expand our sense of connection until one day our society may feel part of a single race in one biosphere.

Another human motivation for empathy is a biological response to altruism (Kohn, 1990). Acting on another's behalf can activate areas of the brain associated with pleasure and reward and release the chemical dopamine (Pavlovich & Krahnke, 2012). This release of dopamine can become a motivating factor when considering the choice of action and may drive empathic behaviors.

In considering the situation Sammy was in on stage, I believe all three factors were probably at play in some form. Lily's holding Sammy's hand certainly protected him from being an outcast of the group, supporting elements of the first two points. Additionally, through the smiles and tears from my wife and me, I believe that Lily was chemically rewarded for her actions, which supports the third point.

Empathy, although extremely beneficial, requires a large amount of cognitive and emotional energy. It takes significantly less energy to walk by a homeless man or even just give him a coin than it does to take on his emotional needs. Given that humans only have a limited amount of reserve for complex cognitive activities (Rock, 2007), people often choose (consciously or subconsciously) to avoid some empathic situations to save energy for other things. Over the past

12 years working in corporate innovation and facilitating the creative problem solving process, I have seen innovation teams decline to create empathic connections with end users due to the time and energy required.

Additionally, suppressed empathy can be a learned response. Similar to theories that education systems suppress natural creative abilities (Robinson, 2011), there are theories that the corporate workplace can suppress acts of empathy. It is not necessarily a conscious effort to discourage empathy, but the act of setting business boundaries, rewarding based on performance, and pretending that our personal lives do not make their way into our work sets up most adults to experience a "game dynamic" (SEEK Company, 2014). [Full disclosure: I am a former SEEK Company associate.]

Game dynamic is a subconscious suppression of both contagious and cognitive empathy in order to continue performing under the assumed guidelines of a workplace (SEEK Company, 2014). We see it in a field reporter who suppresses the urge to stop reporting on her current story when a high-speed car crash happens behind her. We see it when a brand manager chooses to sit on the other side of a one-way mirror when gaining consumer opinions of their products. This form of empathy avoidance is common because humans do not have the stamina required to connect empathically with every individual, and it is normal to turn empathy off and on (Gnaulati, 2013).

Empathy is hard work. To conserve energy humans have learned to be strategic about when and where to go all in. Sometimes, like in Sammy's story, the empathic opportunity comes and is acted upon quickly. Other times, empathy requires significant, long-term cognitive effort and must be turned on through a series of intentional choices.

These factors underscore empathy's relationship to creativity, and heighten the imperative to deploy it when situations dictate. Amabile (1996) considered creativity as the production of ideas that are both novel and useful. Empathy can play a significant role in creative problem solving by helping to uncover currently unmet needs and designing solutions that will provide the greatest emotional utility.

Engaging Empathy

The first step for the perceiver is to decide to connect with another at an emotional level. While this may seem trivial, it is by far the most important and powerful step. The decision allows your brain to focus on the singular task at hand and deprioritizes other thought processes momentarily (Iacoboni, 2009).

The second step as the perceiver is to identify what the target is feeling. It may seem that there are an unlimited number of emotions and that identifying the right one would be very difficult. Yet research has validated findings by Plutchik (2001) that there is a common set of eight emotions (anger, fear, sadness, disgust, surprise, anticipation, trust, and joy) that vary in intensity and have been experienced by all humans by the age of 25. Additionally, it is not critical that the identification of the emotion is exact. Empathy does not require exact knowledge of feeling or situational understanding. In empathy, being close counts.

It is important to take in all available information to improve your emotional identification. For that, you must look to nonverbal communication from the target. It is estimated that 93% of emotional and attitudinal information is communicated in the form of body language and tone of voice, leaving only 7% to be communicated through words alone (Mehrabian, 1972). In situations when it is important to understand emotions, hearing the target's voice and seeing his or her body language is crucial.

Upon identification of an emotion, you can then work to recall a time that you have felt a similar emotion. It is not critical that you match the situational context of your target but instead match the emotion experienced. This is in slight contrast to some interpretations of "put yourself in their shoes," because it does not require contextual mirroring. Empathy is focused on *emotional* mirroring.

For example, let's say you have decided that you would like to connect to another person who is sharing a story about her mother's death. She appears anxious as she shares this story; your job becomes recalling a time that you felt anxious, not recalling a time that a loved one passed away. The final steps are to consider what your needs were when you experienced that similar emotion, and then to consider what the needs of the target might be now. It will not be a lift-and-drop of your needs onto them, but considering your own situation will inform your instincts and strengthen your ability to form a meaningful solution (Shepherd, 2010).

What Is the Possible Return On Empathy?

By choosing to engage in empathy, perceivers get closer emotionally and biologically to their target. The following three examples illustrate how the decision to be empathic can be life-changing and transformative for all those involved.

Health Care

In 2007, Dr. Yehonatan Turner, working at the Shaare Zedek Medical Center in Jerusalem, conducted an experiment with a group of radiologists (Wendling, 2009). Half of the radiologists in the study received a photo of the patient with a radiology scan when it was sent for expert evaluation; half received the scan without a patient photo. The radiologists did not know they were being studied, and completed their examination of the scan and submitted their individual findings. Radiologists who received the picture included 31% more words, a 33% increase in incidental findings, and a 233% increase in the personal recommendations given. If basing the level of health care received on the quantity of the radiologists' observations, one could conclude that the contagious empathy that was prompted by a photo significantly improved the overall care that the patient received. All of the radiologists who were part of the experiment and completed a follow up survey said they were in favor of including a client's photo as a standard procedure.

Non-profit Fund Raising

In 2013, Crossroads Church in Cincinnati decided to find a way to keep local Cincinnati pools open during the coming summer. To raise funds, the church organized a campaign called "Beans and Rice Week." Churchgoers were asked to spend one week eating only beans and rice. By limiting food consumption, church members would save money that in turn would be donated to the public pools. But more importantly, those who participated would experience a bit of what it was like to live on the diet of much of the world's poor. When the week was over, Crossroads received $377,036, a more than 350% return on the campaign's material and marketing costs (Crossroads, 2013). When the effort was repeated in 2014, more than $500,000 was raised. By allowing the participants to connect empathically both with others in need around the world and with a cause that touched the local community, the church encouraged the problem-solving power of cognitive empathy to create personal and city-wide transformation.

Consumer Packaged Goods

As shared in training materials in 2014, SEEK Company described research that contrasted a traditional methodology using consumer verbatim responses with a longer methodology based on empathic connection. The methodologies produced distinctly different insights about the same set of consumers who are insulin dependent.

The traditional insight focused on forgetfulness: "I know I need to take my insulin before meals at night, but my life is hectic and night times are busy. I often forget it" (SEEK, 2014). Based on that insight, client teams decided it would be best to create an alarm system to help prompt and remind the consumer when to take insulin. Ideas discussed went as far as interrupting a television program with a message sent from an iPhone app designed to help.

The empathic insight emphasized emotional vulnerability: "Taking my insulin is a reminder that I am broken. I don't mind giving it to myself in the morning when I am alone, but at night my family is close by, it feels like a reminder to them that I am broken" (SEEK 2014). Based on this insight, the alarm system seems like a bad idea that could potentially exacerbate the problem. However, without taking the time and energy to understand all of the consumer's emotional information, a company may have continued down the first innovation path, spending millions in product development and marketing resources while only further driving an emotional separation between the consumer and her family. Following the empathic insight would likely lead to a more useful solution that could make a real, long-term impact in the lives of consumers and ultimately lead to increased profits for the corporation.

Empathy in Creative Problem Solving

When further analyzed, all three examples followed the basic tenants of the design thinking or user-centered design ideation processes to solve problems that required a creative solution. The basic tenets of design thinking as taught at Stanford University's Hasso Plattner Institute of Design (commonly called the d.school) are *understand, improve,* and *apply* (Meinel & Leifer, 2011). To arrive at solutions that will affect the lives of others, it is critical to choose a path of empathy when first seeking to understand.

Design thinking and user-centered design processes have been increasingly accepted as a viable problem solving process, with hundreds of success stories shared by companies such as IDEO and Frog (Brown & Katz, 2009; Esslinger, 2009). When compared to traditional ideation methods, the main difference is a strong focus on creating empathy at the start of the journey (Liedtka & Ogilvie, 2011). Doing this can drastically affect how problems are solved and potentially allow for positive change in the world.

Conclusion

Empathy's returns are vast. I was surprised when my daughter Lily reached out to hold Sammy's hand, but I feel as if I now understand why a bit more. Whatever her motivations, she showed me just how easy it could be to choose a path of empathy to help others and solve problems.

Further research is needed to directly compare long-term outcomes when empathy is embraced versus when it is switched off. Such research could provide a more explicit answer as to the return on empathy.

Until that happens, I would like to propose that we ask ourselves: Will you choose to invest in empathy? Will you see the need and reach out to hold hands? I hope you will.

References

Amabile, T. M. (1996). *Creativity in context*. Boulder, CO: Westview Press.

Bernhardt, B. C., & Singer, T. (2012). The neural basis of empathy. *Annual Review of Neuroscience, 35*, 1-23.

Blakeslee, S. (2006, January 10). *Cells that read minds*. Retrieved from http://www.nytimes.com/2006/01/10/science/10mirr.html?pagewanted=all&_r=0

Brown, T., & Katz, B. (2009). *Change by design: How design thinking transforms organizations and inspires innovation*. New York, NY: Harper Business.

Crossroads (2013, April 8). *Beans & rice: The final count* [Video file]. Retrieved from https://www.youtube.com/watch?v=YVkjRYAjgrs

Decety, J. (2010). The neurodevelopment of empathy in humans. *Developmental Neuroscience, 32*(4), 257-267.

Decety, J., Chen, C., Harenski, C., & Kiehl, K. A. (2013). An fMRI study of affective perspective taking in individuals with psychopathy: Imagining another in pain does not evoke empathy. *Frontiers in Human Neuroscience, 7*, 489. doi:10.3389/fnhum.2013.00489

Decety, J., & Jackson, P. L. (2004). The functional architecture of human empathy. *Behavioral and Cognitive Neuroscience Reviews, 3*(2), 71-100.

Esslinger, H. (2009). *A fine line: How design strategies are shaping the future of business*. San Francisco, CA: Jossey-Bass.

Gnaulati, E. (2013). *Back to normal: Why ordinary childhood behavior is mistaken for ADHD, Bipolar Disorder, and Autism Spectrum Disorder.* Boston, MA: Beacon Press.

Greene, R. (2012). *Mastery.* New York, NY: Viking.

Iacoboni, M. (2009). *Mirroring people: The science of empathy and how we connect with others.* New York, NY: Picador.

Kohn, A. (1990). *The brighter side of human nature: Altruism and empathy in everyday life.* New York, NY: Basic Books.

Liedtka, J., & Ogilvie, T. (2011). *Designing for growth: A design thinking tool kit for managers.* New York, NY: Columbia Business School Press.

Mehrabian, A. (1972). *Nonverbal communication.* Chicago, IL: Aldine-Atherton.

Meinel, C., & Leifer, L. (2011). *Design thinking: Understand-improve-apply.* Heidelberg, Germany: Springer-Verlag.

Pavlovich, K., & Krahnke, K. (2012). Empathy, connectedness and organisation. *Journal of Business Ethics, 105*(1), 131-137.

Plutchik, R. (2001). The nature of emotions: Human emotions have deep evolutionary roots, a fact that may explain their complexity and provide tools for clinical practice. *American Scientist, 89*(4), 344-350.

Rifkin, J. (2009). *The empathic civilization: The race to global consciousness in a world in crisis.* New York, NY: Tarcher/Penguin.

Robinson, K. (2011). *Out of our minds: Learning to be creative* [Kindle version]. West Sussex, UK: Capstone.

Rock, D. (2007). *Quiet leadership: Six steps to transforming performance at work.* New York, NY: HarperBusiness.

SEEK Company (2014). Red Door™ preparation [Internal presentation]. Unpublished.

Shepherd, P. (2010). *New self, new world: Recovering our senses in the twenty-first century.* Berkeley, CA: North Atlantic Books.

Wendling, P. (2009). Can a photo enhance a radiologist's report? *Clinical Endocrinology News, 4*(2), 6-9.

Wieseke, J., Geigenmuller, A., & Kraus, F. (2012). On the role of empathy in customer-employee interactions. *Journal of Service Research, 15*(3), 316-331.

Zaki, J., & Ochsner, K. (2012). The neuroscience of empathy: Progress, pitfalls, and promise. *Nature Neuroscience, 15*(5), 675-680.

Zhivotovsky, L. A., Rosenberg, N. A., & Feldman, M. W. (2003). Features of evolution and expansion of modern humans, inferred from genome-wide micro-satellite markers. *The American Journal of Human Genetics, 72*(5), 1171-1186. doi:10.1086/375120

About the Author

Geoff Zoeckler is director of innovation at Kaleidoscope, a consultancy in Cincinnati, Ohio. Driven to use his curiosity to solve complex problems, he earned a Bachelor of Science degree in Chemical Engineering and a Master of Science degree in Creativity. He has applied that combination to lead global workshops on empathy-based innovation with Fortune 100 firms and universities. Ask him about the Like A Girl campaign and the Global Citizen Leader program.

Email: GeoffZoeckler@gmail.com
Websites: www.creativityplayground.com, www.kascope.com
Twitter: @GeoffZoeckler
LinkedIn: www.LinkedIn.com/In/GeoffZoeckler

Master's Project:
http://creativityresearch.blogspot.com/2014/05/training-creative-teams.html

Keynote Presentation: Empathy + Action = World Impact:
http://www.kascope.com/from-empathy-to-world-impact

Is Talking About Curiosity an Entry Point to Explaining Creativity?

Jane Harvey
International Center for Studies in Creativity
SUNY Buffalo State

Abstract

This paper takes into account the complexity of the subject of creativity for non-experts, and suggests curiosity as an approach to introduce and explain creativity. A brief look at the meaning of curiosity, early innate curiosity, and the inconvenience, suppression, and dismissal of curiosity provide parallels for understanding creativity. Supported by research in education and creativity, curiosity is a practical first step toward creativity. Curiosity builds openness, balances critical thinking, and supports a progressive mindset. This paper argues that for the layperson, familiarity with curiosity can lead to a better understanding and realization of creativity.

Is Talking About Curiosity an Entry Point to Explaining Creativity?

Decades of research have resulted in varied opinions, models, and definitions of creativity. But due to this complexity, many non-experts fail to fully grasp the concept. In 2008, Makel and Plucker voiced that because "no one in the field can even define creativity" (p. 248) those outside the field become alienated from what creativity is. Both Day (1968) and Runco (2007) found ambiguity in definitions of creativity. Hennessey and Amabile (2010) found fragmentation in research, lack of consensus, and a wide range of different opinions, methodologies, and perspectives on creativity.

The vastness of the subject persists in making it seem unattainable to the layperson, but creativity must be explained in order to nurture individual creative development and practice. Sawyer (2011) suggested that clarifying creativity "will lead to a more creative society and will enhance the creative potential of our families, our workplaces, and our [educational] institutions" (p. 5). Because creativity is so important, introducing it in a way that can be more easily understood might help people realize their creative potential.

Leaning On Curiosity

Though creativity may feel like something abstract or outside an individual's capacity, curiosity is a familiar concept from childhood. Considering curiosity as an appetizer for creativity can be a practical introduction for both the subject and the practice of creativity. Familiarity with the term "curiosity" eliminates the *art bias* of creativity (Runco, 2007; Sawyer, 2011). The statement "everyone is creative" may not sound believable, but becoming more *curious,* at any age, may seem achievable. Engel (2011) noted that curiosity is second nature to children: "All children, when they are young, are eager to learn more about the unfamiliar" (p. 628). Curiosity is being amazed by the world, filled with wonder, and asking questions—especially "why"—in our search for knowledge and newness. In 2012, Jirout and Klahr proposed a definition of curiosity as "the threshold of desired uncertainty in the environment which leads to exploratory behavior" (p. 157). Csikszentmihalyi (1996) explained that as we age, we lose this sense of wonder and the need to explore diverse interests. He maintained that reigniting curiosity could lead to creativity.

The History of Curiosity

Berlyne (1960), a pioneer in curiosity research, broke curiosity down into four types: the desire to know; the desire to try, experience, and feel; seeking novelty and challenge; and investigating uncertainty or complexity. Negative forms of curiosity are voyeurism, nosiness, lack of self-restraint, and excessive sensation-seeking, such as addiction, risk behavior, and obsession (Kashdan, Rose, & Fincham, 2004). This paper refers to curiosity broadly, inclusive of responsible and positive intellectual curiosity, inquiry, and a sense of wonder.

If we consider the use of curiosity as the stepping-stone toward creativity, we should acknowledge that curiosity got stepped on in the past. Curiosity's negative side traces back to biblical and mythological stories of forbidden knowledge (Harrison, 2001). Many cultures—as well as parenting and leadership styles—suppressed curiosity with authority, conformity, repression, fear, and religion (Davis, 2004). Asking questions is often still seen as disrespectful or defiant. Curiosity carries a long history of being viewed as a vice; excessive desire for knowledge went beyond what was necessary, was useless and vain (Harrison, 2001). Benedict (2001) brought to light how dangerous curiosity was if "ungoverned" (p. 237), and "intellectual restlessness" was a morally offensive ambition of overstepping boundaries (p. 246). Appreciating curiosity's history and negative baggage help in understanding the challenges of practicing creativity.

The emergence of modern science in the 16th and 17th centuries redeemed curiosity. Experimentation and observation led to knowledge of the world. During the Renaissance, many of the wealthy maintained private collections of interesting natural findings. "Cabinets of curiosity" were early mini-museums, based on a fascination with nature. The need to understand our world inspired observation and study in science. Older references to curiosity mostly refer to scientific exploration and research (Ball, 2013). Inquiries about the natural world led to academic discoveries, new resources, and new lands. Eventually, curiosity turned to the observation of human behavior. Psychology and social sciences, which encompass the science of creativity, began with curiosity about people (Loewenstein, 1994; Runco & Albert, 2010).

Curiosity, the Introduction to Creativity

Based on 50 years of extensive research of creativity, Torrance believed curiosity was the key to creativity (Torrance & Safter, 1990). There are numerous examples of empirical research stating that curiosity leads to essential components of creativity, including:

- intrinsic motivation (Amabile, 1997; Sternberg, 1988)

- imagining (Davis, 2004; Torrance & Safter, 1999)

- novelty (Davis, 2004; Day, 1968; Puccio, Mance, & Murdock, 2011)

- personal fulfillment (Csikszentmihalyi, 1996; Maslow, 1970; Rogers, 1963)

- mindfulness (Kashdan, 2010; Langer, 1997)

Other effects of curiosity that have been researched include:

- health and wellbeing (Atkinson & Joyce, 2011)

- openness (Kashdan, Rose, & Fincham 2004; Kaufman, 2013)

- tolerance for complexity (Davis, 2004; Day, 1968; Kashdan et al., 2004)

- tolerance for ambiguity (Kashdan, et al., 2004; Puccio et al., 2011; Sternberg, 1988; Torrance & Safter, 1999)

- playfulness (Csikszentmihalyi, 1997; Taylor & Rogers, 2001)

- risk-taking (Kurtzman, 1967)

- experimentation (Torrance & Safter, 1999)

- emotional intelligence (Leonard & Harvey, 2007)

- flow (Csikszentmihalyi, 1996)

In addition, Maw and Magoon (1971) found highly curious children were more creative and had greater social responsibility. In 2011, Von Stumm, Hell, and Chamorro-Premuzic noted that students with high curiosity performed better academically. Based on all these academic findings, it makes practical sense to connect people to creativity by reconnecting them to curiosity first.

Curiosity Is Part of Creativity

Curiosity encourages life-long learning and development, staying current on trends, and maintaining a growth mindset. Despite the process of aging, we can reform, refresh, and rethink. Csikszentmihalyi (1996) stressed, "Curiosity is about being open to the world around you" (p. 160). Taking an interest in our world is part of living life fully. Kashdan (2010) asserted that curiosity connects to the human need to belong, find meaning, and achieve confidence. He believes that spirituality, achievement, and creativity all relate to curiosity. Curiosity is the connector, making life meaningful, insightful, and satisfying. Building on that view, perhaps practicing curiosity will kindle more social innovation and engagement and less apathy. Kashdan (2010) remarked, "When we are curious, we see things differently; we use our powers of observation more fully. We sense what is happening in the present moment" (5 Benefits of an Inquiring Mind section, para. 2).

Child development is fueled by efforts to understand what is unknown, and children use inquiry to try to make sense of their world (Engel, 2011). Trying to make sense of anything extends well beyond childhood. For adults, the constancy of change and progress requires ongoing learning and questioning. Staying open and absorbing multiple perspectives, and not giving up during problem solving helps us to find meaning and solutions. Curiosity begins with uncertainty and leads to openness through exploration and newness. Harriman & Mauzy (2003) suggested that continual exposure to unknowns strengthens resistance to our fear of newness. An adult can "inoculate him- or herself against the loss of curiosity" with practiced openness (p. 41).

Making mistakes, appearing less than competent, or feeling inferior is frightening. Uncertainty feels uncomfortable, and unknowns are unwanted. We often choose the safest route forward to avoid risk to ourselves (Hennessey, 2010; Moran, 2010). Creativity, however, requires a willingness to take risks. In order to help individuals see risks as challenges and not threats, curiosity must be supported (Beghetto, 2010). As we encourage and cultivate the willingness for risk-taking, curiosity, open-mindedness, playfulness, and exploration of wide interests, we head towards creativity (Davis, 2004).

Growing Curiosity

Rogers (1963) encouraged freedom for curiosity, exploration, and openness to experience as ways to develop creativity. The freedom to follow what interests us cultivates curiosity. In childhood, curiosity is natural and encouraged. Children's play provides adventure for learning (Ball, 2013). Play, imagination, and being unproductive are acceptable investments of time during childhood. Responsible adults monitor and provide safety, even protecting children from their curiosity. In teaching the ways of the world, adult control can shut down questioning and exploration. Instilling discipline, self-control, and conformity will quiet and suffocate curiosity. Many adults find exploration to be wasteful and risky, and find questioning to be interruptive. Chak (2007) found that negative adult responses and expectations hindered children's curiosity. Engel (2011) noticed very young children investigating, exploring, questioning, and desiring new information, but found a "stunning lack of such inquiry in school-aged children" (p. 634). Kim (2011) contended younger children are becoming "more narrow-minded, less intellectually curious and less open to new experiences" (p. 292). Adults stand over and disgorge information while the child sits below and fills up with knowledge and lessons. If knowledge output overshadows free time for building on new knowledge, and time for discussion is cut out, students will disengage (Kim, 2011). Stokoe (2012) claimed students lose interest because they stop asking questions, and "as we grow up, we start believing the answers are more important than the questions" (p. 63).

All ages benefit from cognitive freedom for questioning, stretching thought, exploring, and breaking barriers. Openness and learning to look at new and different perspectives are elements of creativity. In today's world, there is a great emphasis on being an expert and having strong opinions, but we have to remain open to "unknowing" and learning beyond our expertise. By staying too set on perfecting our specialty, we miss the opportunity for personal expansion and growth (Csikszentmihalyi, 1996). If we can ask "why" more, we get connected to others' ideas that differ from ours. Empathy is gained by taking time to wonder what it's like in someone else's shoes. Curiosity interconnects differences among others. Koranda and Sheehan (2014) found curiosity led to higher emotional intelligence when people observed and interacted with others. Curiosity's openness allows us to listen, try new things, face change and the unknown, and dismiss the need to be right (Davis, 2004). We would achieve greater harmony if people learned to notice differences based in curiosity, not out of judgment and prejudice.

If curiosity involves wanting to know more beyond what we already know, it is hard to imagine that we abandoned curiosity in childhood. Or did we? The Renaissance *"habit" of curiosity* was about collecting things of interest (Benedict, 2001). That same habit of curiosity in the modern day is our use of Pinterest and other social media (Cesare, 2014). We can wander the Internet to learn about the world with YouTube, TED talks, and global news feeds, and we can store and share large collections of our interests digitally. Depending on our enthusiasms and "need to know," curiosity is either seeking deeper knowledge or cruising along at a surface level. Willingham (2014) termed *short-term curiosity* as when our interest is piqued by something, yet transient. Short-term curiosity is only a sampling. Skimming information is common today. How deep are we willing to look and how much time are we willing to give? Information is everywhere and is readily accessible. That might make it appear like all the answers are quick to find, so we don't have to explore or spend much effort thinking for ourselves. Willingham (2014) noted that personal technology might be interrupting curiosity and learning. Access to easy answers, instant gratification, and mental boredom have students putting out less effort to problem solve. Though "curiosity entails a willingness to engage in mental work" (Willingham, 2014, p. 35), students may not get enough pleasure from solving a problem. Leslie (2014) noted that while the Internet provides more opportunity to learn, it might also be a demotivator and give people an excuse not to try too hard to do so.

A Curiously Critical Balance

Creativity requires a balance of divergent and convergent thinking (Osborn, 1953), but the focus on structured critical thinking in current education teaches only half of the creative process. We need to build in time for curiosity. Our culture seems to value structure and doing versus depth of thinking. We expect speed and efficiency, but curious inquiry needs time for additional questions and exploration. Over-scheduling and pushing ourselves and our children toward focused expertise squeezes out free time for playing with thoughts and ideas.

Kashdan (2011) suggested there is a misalignment of aspiration and actual outcomes occurring in our schools:

> If we want kids to experience a sense of wonder and discover new information on their own (curiosity), if we want them to generate novel, adaptive ideas (creativity), and if we want them to derive their own perspectives and conclusions after a discussion (critical thinking), then the current educational system is a failure. (para. 4)

As a balance to critical thinking, unexpected ideas must be welcome, explored, and not dismissed (Beghetto, 2010). If teachers invited students' curious thinking, they might gain insight, connections, and new teaching strategies. Nickerson (1999) proposed that teachers should tolerate detours, disruptions, diversions, and have children experience curiosity as well as its consequences. Students thrive from dialog with their teachers and should be encouraged to question things. Engel (2009) stressed the imbalance of teachers' questions: those that are built to test knowledge weigh heavier than those that are meant to extend learning and promote further inquiry. Torrance & Safter (1990) saw curiosity as a way for teachers and students to co-experience learning. Supporting curiosity and teaching creativity are critical for education and adulthood (Johnson, Blum, & Giedd, 2009).

Curiosity in the Brain

According to Engel (2011) "When children are curious, they learn. It turns out that curiosity in school is not merely a nicety but a necessity" (p. 628). Maw and Maw (1961) showed that children with high curiosity learned and remembered what they learned longer than less curious children. Amabile's (1997) research on intrinsic motivation suggested that deep interest and curiosity drive creativity.

Research by Gruber, Gelman, and Ranganath (2014) demonstrated that curiosity puts the brain into a learning state, preparing it to make new connections and to retain information for memory. In the brain, anticipation and curiosity cause the release of dopamine. Their study found that a brain warmed up with curiosity retains information better. Intrigue for certain information chemically creates a kind of halo of engagement.

Long before tools such as those used by Gruber et al. (2014) were being used to study brain chemistry, Torrance (1993) had identified curiosity as an effective lure for anticipatory learning. He considered teaching as creating "the desire to know, to learn, or to discover; to arouse curiosity; to stimulate the imagination, and to give purpose and motivation" (p. 233). The first stage of Torrance's Incubation Model of Teaching is "heightening anticipation" creating the desire in students to find out and understand (Torrance & Safter, 1990). Additionally, Torrance stressed learning with elements of curiosity: looking deeper into new information, using awareness, and practicing openness. In essence, Torrance's model supported creative learning by introducing curiosity.

Curiosity Serves Creativity

Both children and adults seek to observe and make sense of the world. Collaboration and curiosity enable us to learn from each other because we all think differently. Curiosity about others enables us to be more tolerant. Getting beyond ourselves gets us beyond our individual perspectives. When teachers support experimentation, embracing failure and divergent thinking, they teach "new ways of seeing the world" (Sheridan-Rabideau, 2010, p. 58). Curiosity is what drives both science and art in the search to find meaning in our world.

Berlyne (1960) proposed that curiosity is a desire for change and novelty. Novelty can be unpredictable, but we must rediscover our attraction to it (Csikszentmihalyi, 1996). Curiosity fades when our lives are routine, task-oriented, or too idle. However, predictability provides safety, security, comfort, and a sense of control. As we are increasingly dependent on using data to support evidence-based decisions, it will take more than passive curiosity to see future possibilities. Novelty, uncertainty, and progress will require active curiosity. Puccio et al. (2011) proposed that those who see novelty as a possibility for the future may realize why thinking differently is beneficial. Sharpening awareness and asking more questions is a start.

Conclusion

Davis (2004) asserted that "high curiosity is a classic creative trait" (p. 90). Curiosity might even be the fast lane for creativity. Due to the ambiguity and complexity surrounding creativity, I suggest that curiosity might be a simpler, more understandable way to start practicing creativity. We must get beyond our individual experiences to face future situations, confront new beliefs and embrace different perspectives. Being interested enough to care, and having a familiarity with curiosity can guide transformation to creative thinking. If we extend the value and support for curiosity beyond early childhood, into education and the workplace, more people may start to embrace and practice it. This retrieval and renewal of curiosity can lead to a beginning understanding and realization of creativity for non-experts.

References

Amabile, T. M. (1997). Motivating creativity in organizations: On doing what you love and loving what you do. *California Management Review, 40*(1), 39-58.

Atkinson, S., & Joyce, K. E. (2011). The place and practices of well-being in local governance. *Environment and Planning C: Government and Policy 29*, 133-148.

Ball, P. (2013). *Curiosity: How science became interested in everything.* Chicago, IL: University of Chicago Press.

Beghetto, R. A. (2010). Nurturing creativity in the classroom. In J. C. Kaufman & R. J. Sternberg (Eds.), *The Cambridge handbook of creativity* (pp. 447-463). New York, NY: Cambridge University Press.

Benedict, B. M. (2001). *Curiosity: A cultural history of early modern inquiry.* Chicago, IL: University of Chicago Press.

Berlyne, D. E. (1960). *Conflict, arousal, and curiosity.* New York, NY: McGraw-Hill.

Cabra, J. F., & Uribe, D. (2013). Creative Behavior. In E. Carayannis, I. Dubina, N. Seel, D. F. J. Campbell, & D. Uzunidis (Eds.), *Encyclopedia on creativity, invention, innovation and entrepreneurship* (pp. 267-271). New York, NY: Springer.

Cesare, C. (2014). The habit of curiosity. *Agathos: An International Review of the Humanities & Social Sciences, 5*(1),83-99.

Chak, A. (2007). Teachers' and parents' conceptions of children's curiosity and exploration. *International Journal of Early Years Education, 15*(2), 141-159. doi:10.1080/09669760701288690

Csikszentmihalyi, M. (1996). *Creativity: Flow and the psychology of discovery and invention*. New York, NY: HarperCollins.

Csikszentmihalyi, M. (1997). *Finding flow: The psychology of engagement with everyday life*. New York, NY: Basic Books.

Davis, G. A. (2004). *Creativity is forever* (5th ed.). Dubuque, IA: Kendall/Hunt.

Day, H. (1968). A curious approach to creativity. *Canadian Psychologist, 9*(4), 485-497. doi:10.1037/h0082675

Engel, S. (2009). Is curiosity vanishing? *Journal of the American Academy of Child and Adolescent Psychiatry, 48*(8), 777-779. doi:10.1097/CHI.0b013e3181aa03b0

Engel, S. (2011). Children's need to know: Curiosity in schools. *Harvard Educational Review, 81*(4), 625-646.

Gruber, M. J., Gelman, B. D., & Ranganath, C. (2014). States of curiosity modulate hippocampus-dependent learning via the dopaminergic circuit. *Neuron, 84*(2), 486-496. doi:10.1016/j.neuron.2014.08.060

Harriman, R. A., & Mauzy, J. (2003). *Creativity, Inc.: Building an inventive organization*. Boston, MA: Harvard Business Press.

Harrison, P. (2001). Curiosity, forbidden knowledge, and the reformation of natural philosophy in early modern England. *History of Science Society, 92*(2), 265-290.

Hennessey, B. A. (2010). The creativity-motivation connection. In J. C. Kaufman & R. J. Sternberg (Eds.), *The Cambridge handbook of creativity* (pp. 342-365). New York, NY: Cambridge University Press.

Hennessey, B. A., & Amabile, T. M. (2010). Creativity. *Annual Review of Psychology, 61*, 569-598. doi:10.1146/annurev.psych.093008.100416

Jirout, J. & Klahr, D. (2012). Children's scientific curiosity: In search of an operational definition of an elusive concept. *Developmental Review, 32*(12), 125–160. doi:10.1016/j.dr.2012.04.002

Johnson, S. B., Blum, R. W., & Giedd, J. N. (2009). Adolescent maturity and the brain: The promise and pitfalls of neuroscience research in adolescent health policy. *Journal of Adolescent Health, 45*(3), 216–221. doi:10.1016/j. jadohealth.2009.05.016

Kashdan, T. (2010, May). *The power of curiosity*. Retrieved from http:// experiencelife.com/article/the-power-of-curiosity

Kashdan, T. B. (2011, May 11). *3 ideas to prevent schools from killing creativity, curiosity, and critical thinking* [Blog post]. Retrieved from http://www. psychologytoday.com/blog/curious/201105/3-ideas-prevent-schools-killing-creativity-curiosity-and-critical-thinking

Kashdan, T. B., Rose, P., & Fincham, F. D. (2004). Curiosity and exploration: Facilitating positive subjective experiences and personal growth opportunities. *Journal of Personality Assessment, 82*(3), 291-305. doi:10.1207/s15327752jpa8203_05

Kaufman, S. B. (2013). Opening up openness to experience: A four-factor model and relations to creative achievement in the arts and sciences. *The Journal of Creative Behavior, 47*(4), 233–255. doi:10.1002/jocb.33

Kim, K. H. (2011). The creativity crisis: The decrease in creative thinking scores on the Torrance Tests of Creative Thinking. *Creativity Research Journal, 23*(4), 285–295. doi:10.1080/10400419.2011.627805

Koranda, D., & Sheehan, K. B. (2014). Teaching curiosity: An essential advertising skill? *Journal of Advertising Education, 18*(1), 13-24.

Kurtzman, K. A. (1967). A study of school attitudes, peer acceptance, and personality of creative adolescents. *Exceptional Children, 34*, 157-162.

Langer, E. J. (1997). *The power of mindful learning*. Reading, MA: Addison Wesley.

Leonard, N. H., & Harvey, M. (2007). The trait of curiosity as a predictor of emotional intelligence. *Journal of Applied Social Psychology, 37*(7), 1545-1561. doi10.1111/j.1559-1816.2007.00226.x

Leslie, I. (2014). *Curious: The desire to know and why your future depends on it*. New York, NY: Basic Books.

Loewenstein, G. (1994). The psychology of curiosity: A review and reinterpretation. *Psychological Bulletin, 116*(1), 75-98. doi:10.1037//0033-2909.116.1.75

Makel, M. C., & Plucker, J. A. (2008). Creativity. In S. I. Pfeifer (Ed.), *Handbook of giftedness in children* (pp. 247-270). New York, NY: Springer.

Maslow, A. (1970). *Motivation and personality*. New York, NY: Harper & Row.

Maw, W. H., & Magoon, A. J. (1971). The curiosity dimension of fifth-grade children: A factorial discriminant analysis. *Child Development, 42*(6), 2023-2031.

Maw, W. H., & Maw, E. W. (1961). Information recognition by children with high and low curiosity. *Educational Research Bulletin, 40*(8), 197-201.

Moran, S. (2010). The roles of creativity in society. In J. C. Kaufman & R. J. Sternberg (Eds.), *The Cambridge handbook of creativity* (pp. 74-90). New York, NY: Cambridge University Press.

Nickerson, R. S. (1999). Enhancing creativity. In R. J. Sternberg (Ed.), *Handbook of creativity.* Cambridge, UK: Cambridge University Press.

Osborn, A. F. (1953). *Applied imagination.* New York, NY: Charles Scribner's Sons.

Puccio, G. J., Mance, M., & Murdock, M. C. (2011). *Creative leadership: Skills that drive change* (2nd ed.). Thousand Oaks, CA: Sage.

Rogers, C. R. (1963). The concept of the fully functioning person. *Psychotherapy, 1*(1), 17-26. doi:10.1037/h0088567

Runco, M. A. (2007). *Creativity: Theories and themes: Research, development, and practice.* Detroit, MI: Thomson Gale.

Runco, M. A., & Albert, R. S. (2010). Creativity research: A historical view. In J. C. Kaufman & R. J. Sternberg (Eds.), *The Cambridge handbook of creativity* (pp. 3-19). New York, NY: Cambridge University Press.

Sawyer, R. K. (2011). *Explaining creativity: The science of human innovation.* New York, NY: Oxford University Press.

Sheridan-Rabideau, M. (2010). Creativity repositioned. *Arts Education Policy Review, 111*, 54-58. doi:10.1080/10632910903455876

Sternberg, R. J. (1988). *The nature of creativity: Contemporary psychological perspectives.* New York, NY: Cambridge University Press.

Stokoe, R. (2012). Curiosity, a condition for learning. *The International Schools Journal, 32*(1) 63-66.

Taylor, S. I., & Rogers, C. S. (2001). The relationship between playfulness and creativity of Japanese preschool children. *International Journal of Early Childhood, 33*(1), 43-49.

Torrance, E. P. (1993). Understanding creativity: Where to start? *Psychological Inquiry, 4*(3), 232-234.

Torrance, E. P., & Safter, H. T. (1990). *The incubation model of teaching.* Buffalo, NY: Bearly Limited.

Torrance, E. P., & Safter, H. T. (1999). *Making the creative leap beyond.* Buffalo, NY: Creative Education Foundation.

Von Stumm, S., Hell, B., & Chamorro-Premuzic, T. (2011). The hungry mind: Intellectual curiosity is the third pillar of academic performance. *Perspectives on Psychological Science, 6*(6), 574-588. doi:10.1177/1745691611421204

Willingham, D. (2014). Making students more curious. *Knowledge Quest, 42*(5), 32-35.

About the Author

Jane Harvey is an insightful designer, graphic recorder, artist, and visual facilitator. She holds a B.F.A. from Parsons School of Design and an M.S. in Creativity from the International Center for Studies in Creativity at SUNY Buffalo State. Her master's project is an engaging book on creativity, produced in collaboration with Kathryn P. Haydon.

Website: www.visualtranslating.com
Twitter: @art_jhg
LinkedIn: linkedin.com/pub/jane-harvey/28/786/544

How Does Playfulness Affect Adult Learning?

Juliana Sánchez-Trujillo
Universidad de la Sabana
Bogota, Colombia

Erica Swiatek
Innovate Faster
Buffalo, New York

Abstract

Adult education must accommodate people who have short attention spans and who struggle to memorize content. By integrating several learning techniques such as flexibility, adaptation, and the use of imagination into facilitated activities that encourage problem solving, playfulness presents an opportunity to ease and accelerate learning. As a natural process that provides social and cognitive benefits, play makes learning more enjoyable and effective. Although adult learners have usually been taught that play is a waste of time and lacks seriousness, research suggests they learn better through direct experience, and play complements that process. Play also aids learning because it provides the opportunity to make connections with real-life experiences in a safe environment that promotes the development of higher-order thinking skills.

How Does Playfulness Affect Adult Learning?

T he goal of post-compulsory education and training is to provide people with the tools needed to thrive in different environments. This sector integrates teachers, trainers, and learners in schools, universities, and workplaces (Eastwood, Coates, Dixon, & Harvey, 2009). The learning environment is complex; these adult learners have different individual needs and goals. Some of them are required to take classes, for example, while others choose to attend out of personal interest. In both cases, the instructor or professor has to provide a variety of methodologies and exercises that will potentially help participants to acquire new knowledge.

However, traditional methods based on repetition, passively listening to the instructor, and standardized education no longer provide expected results (Meier 2000). Particularly in training, it is very common to find difficulties transferring knowledge to the workplace (Coyle, Hood, & Marsh, 2010; Kolb, 1994; Meier, 2000). These issues emerge because the learning process is no longer significant to the participant, and the required information is not properly stored. In some cases, transferring theory to real-life experience turns out to be impossible. For example, when training customer service soft skills, the theory needs to be internalized by the participant so that he or she will be unconsciously skilled, meaning that these skills are available in real time when needed (Puccio, Mance, & Murdock, 2011). If that training is not supported with, for instance, real scenarios during training, it will be hard for the learner to transfer theory to real customers.

New technologies have transformed learning and working, yet at the same time, they have posed challenges that require flexibility and creativity on the part of educators. For instance, while most of Generation Y (born between 1980-2000) and all of Generation Z (2000-present), have been exposed to digital technology from birth (Coyle et al., 2010), other generations may have difficulties adapting to the same technologies. At the same time, it is common to find work teams located in different time zones, which has engendered the need to use virtual environments for both collaboration and training. Furthermore, time constraints affect the learning process; there is often little time and a lot of content to be covered. All these developments demand learning spaces and experiences that will allow the participant to learn, transfer, and apply new knowledge rapidly. This paper asserts that playfulness can contribute to enhancing the educational experience for adult learners.

What Is Playfulness?

Defining play is oddly challenging because everyone has experienced it in some way. Given its strong connection to games, what we mean by "play" may be misconstrued. However, if one is asked to think about "playful" activities, different ideas may come to mind because the term has a broader perspective.

Play can be understood as a freestanding activity that exists for its own sake (Huizinga, 1968). It is separate from ordinary activity, and generates intense feelings of joy and flow, which Csikszentmihalyi (1991) characterized as losing track of time, being fully emerged in the activity, and feeling intrinsically motivated. That is why Brown and Vaughn (2009) held that "play is a state of mind, rather than an activity" (p. 60).

Huizinga (1968) observed that playful activity must meet five criteria. First, it must be free, not imposed. Second, it must allow the participant to escape his or her own reality. Third, it requires time and space limits, which can be repeated. Fourth, it demands order; it requires a beginning and an end. Finally, playful activities must have their own rules.

Playfulness affects cognitive, social, and physical aspects of a person's life. However, culturally, play is only widely accepted in regards to children; it may be seen as frivolous, a waste of time, and lacking seriousness when it involves older participants. This belief persists despite research that indicates lack of play is equivalent to sleep deprivation (Panksepp & Beatty, 1980), in the sense that it impairs memory and cognitive functions. Indeed, Brown and Vaughan (2009) note that "the opposite of play is not work—the opposite of play is depression" (p. 126).

Play is a natural process both in humans and animals, and its importance lies in the benefits it provides for both social and cognitive development. Because learning is a lifelong skill, these benefits are not exclusive to children. People of all ages who play may enjoy the benefits of enhanced creativity and problem solving, social cohesiveness, decision making, well-being, adaptation, and improved learning (Brown & Vaughan, 2009). Play also contributes to healthy brain development (Rosenzweig, Bennett, & Diamond, 1969).

In play, "we see things in a different way and have fresh insights" (Brown & Vaughan, 2009, p. 17), which helps us be more creative and solve problems in novel and useful ways. This is vitally important in a world that constantly demands solutions to new and difficult challenges. Educators need to facilitate knowledge in a way that prepares people to adapt to change, think creatively, solve challenges, and implement solutions. In short, they need to engage in creative thinking, which is in turn linked to the development of curiosity.

Curiosity promotes exploration, higher academic performance, and improved intelligence (Von Stumm, Hell, & Chamorro-Premuzic, 2011). Play rewards curiosity and extends it to data gathering and then to experimenting and problem solving.

Play opens doors to the learning that allows participants to explore, use imagination, and be more optimistic (Brown & Vaughan, 2009). Moreover, it permits learning and development in ways that can adapt to individual learning styles. "People prefer to learn creatively by exploring, questioning, manipulating, rearranging things, testing and modifying, listening, looking, feeling and then thinking about it" (Torrance & Safter, 1990, p. 13).

In other words, play complements learning by making it an enjoyable activity that gets lessons across. This does not mean that the professor or instructor must become an entertainer, but a facilitator of knowledge that brings fun back to learning. For some educators, this point of view may require a revision in the way they approach the profession: "Play isn't the enemy of learning, it's learning's partner. Play is like fertilizer for brain growth" (Brown & Vaughan, 2009, p. 101).

Linking Playfulness and Adult Learning

Human beings have a lifelong necessity to learn, but the ways in which they do it varies significantly depending on age. For that reason, the discipline of *andragogy* was created as a means to study adult learning needs and ways to put theory into practice. This approach is different from *pedagogy* (teaching methods used for children K-12) because it involves self-directed and autonomous learners, and teachers as facilitators of learning (Henschke, 2009; Knowles, 1984; Merriam, 2001).

Learning is a process, one that may begin in the classroom or a meeting room or even a shopping mall. It is enhanced by our experiences and domain knowledge. Therefore, it is important that anyone associated with adult learning realize that learning is a process and not just about instant outcomes (Kolb, 1984).

In addition, it is not enough to consider learning without integrating thinking and problem-solving skills. In order to identify the skills that need to be involved in the learning process, Bloom and Krathwohl (1956; updated by Anderson & Krathwohl, 2001) categorized six different thinking processes by complexity.

These levels are organized in two different dimensions: lower-order thinking (remembering, understanding, and applying) and higher-order thinking (analyzing, evaluating, and creating), and both are integral to effective learning (Coyle et al., 2010). Some people are able to move easily to high-order thinking skills (Von Stumm et al., 2011) which helps them to be more open minded, expand their knowledge, and put their creativity skills to use. Creativity requires synthesis to connect the unconscious of the imagination with rational thinking skills (Puccio et al., 2011). When integrating play in the learning process, learners can easily move from one stage to the other while enjoying the process.

However, in order to be open to learning, adults—much more so than children—need to understand the importance of what is being taught. They desire to be seen as responsible people who can make their own decisions and who need to have learning experiences centered in real-life problems or tasks that can be effectively solved. At the same time, the instructor needs to be mindful of the fact that adults come to training or class with previous knowledge and experiences (Knowles, 1984; Meier, 2000). Therefore, the educator's goal is to help adult learners build on and make connections to what they already know.

For adult learners to be effective, they need to use their skills. Kolb (1984) identified four essential abilities required of adult learners: concrete experience, reflective observation, abstract conceptualization, and active experimentation. Collaboration is another skill that can assist adult learners. Meier (2000) emphasized the benefit of collaborative learning: "A genuine learning community is always better for learning than a collection of isolated individuals" (p. 9).

However, theory alone is not enough. Providing a safe environment is also crucial in the process. The environment needs to be positive, safe, and socially engaging (Gagnon & Collay, 2001; Meier, 2000).

Curiosity and motivation play a big part in the learning process as well. The classroom is similar to a buffet, where the person chooses those things he or she wishes to eat. In learning, the classroom or lesson also offers a variety of information and insights that are to be chosen by the participant. Adult learners in particular have selective memory and attention, and therefore, they will only select those things they consider significant (Jensen, 1998; Meier, 2000; Merriam, 2001). Therefore, the more the participant enjoys the process, the higher the quality and quantity of learning that will occur. In the words of Meier (2000):

> This "joy" means interest, connectedness, and the involved and happy creation of meaning and understanding and value on the part of the learner. It's the joy of giving birth to something new. And this joy is far more significant for learning than any technique or method or medium you might choose to use. (p. xii)

Kolb (1984) agreed on the role of relatedness in encouraging learning: "Knowledge is the result of the transaction between social knowledge and personal knowledge" (p. 36). Therefore, it is helpful when designing lessons for adults to include opportunities for them to work with each other and share their experiences as well as to reflect with facilitated questions. Meier (2000), who pioneered the concept of accelerated learning, believes that the adult learner cannot passively absorb information. The learner needs to be immersed and to create something in order to become engaged with the content. This process requires total involvement, and includes a continual process of feedback, reflection, evaluation, and reimmersion.

A second powerful adult learning theory, constructionism, is based on thinking with and through concrete objects. This theory suggests when we construct something external to ourselves we gain knowledge by creating images in our minds (Edwards, 1986; Kristiansen & Rasmussen, 2014). The research associated with this theory shows that the use of objects aids the inquiry process by making the hidden thought evident and discussable. This approach is also supported by the scientific brain-hand connection research indicating that 80% of brain cells are connected to the hands (Wilson, 2010).

To take advantage of constructionist strategies, instructors need to involve learners in activities that allow them to think through their hands in order to reach deeper insights. Examples of these activities include drawing, making collages, creating sculptures, building with LEGOs, working on junk inventions, etc. In addition, when using hands-on activities to create prototypes or models, pictures can be taken and used to bring learners back into a state of playfulness, allowing the instructor to build on previous concepts easily.

One important way that instructors can emphasize connections between concepts is through a debriefing held at the end of a session. Many instructors fall short in their class design and delivery because they skip or skimp on this essential part of the learning process. Even playful activities often feel meaningless to learners without a proper review. Gagnon and Collay (2001), whose studies focused on learner connectivity at the social, cognitive, and unconscious levels, suggested that debriefing is crucial to ensuring lasting connections. They note that it makes learning more concrete, as the instructor uses guiding questions to bring together the reflections that have occurred throughout the learning experience. "Reflection should be a rewarding and positive process which starts and ends with a resourceful state of mind and springboards you to further enhance your practice" (Gagnon & Collay, 2001, p. 157).

The debriefing portion of the learning should be a celebration. Some participants may struggle to think of more than one thing that they learned in the lesson.

Learners can be encouraged to think in more detail about that single thing (Gagnon & Collay, 2001).

Debriefing has another powerful benefit: it encourages the learner to keep thinking about the content and discussion that occurred in class, which leads to incubation. Incubation, which allows reflection time, plays a part in the process of learning as well. It allows for an idea or concept to be processed by the subconscious. According to Torrance (1979), incubation requires abilities, skills, and motivation. These can be activated by the instructional procedures and conditions. Incubation provides learners a way to take the learning to a higher-order thinking process that goes beyond logical and rational thought processes. However, it is important to be mindful that this process requires time. Therefore, instructors should provide the time and space to do it, but not force it.

Conclusion

Play is vital to learning because it provides a safe environment where participants can experiment, make pretend decisions, and connect the new knowledge with their own reality. It also gives learners the opportunity to involve hands and minds, allowing for deeper connections and experiences that last even after the classroom experience has concluded.

If a learner experiences play in the classroom, they may find themselves in a state of flow or joy. This can encourage them to take risks, collaborate more effectively, and dive into the social aspects of learning that offer so many benefits.

As instructors build playful activities into their lessons, it is important to remember and respect that adult learners might resist these activities at first. Learners have been taught that play is a frivolous waste of time. When using these techniques, instructors may find it helps to explain how and why play will benefit them in their learning.

However, instructors need to be mindful that incorporating play in the learning process should not be an excuse to sit back and relax. There are times when standing in front of the class is the best way to deliver educational content. For that reason, lessons need to be planned in a way that balances both experiential and traditional teaching and training methods.

Finally, it is very important to understand that playing without a purpose does not accelerate the learning process. In order to use it as a teaching strategy, it must be supported by exercises that allow the learner to reflect on what happened, why it is important, and how to transfer the new knowledge to his or her personal and professional lives.

References

Anderson, L. W., & Krathwohl, D. (Eds.). (2001). *A taxonomy for learning, teaching, and assessing: A revision of Bloom's Taxonomy of Educational Objectives*. New York, NY: Longman.

Bloom, B. S., & Krathwohl, D. R. (1956). *Taxonomy of educational objectives: The classification of educational goals. Handbook I: Cognitive domain*. New York, NY: Longman.

Brown, S., & Vaughan, C. (2009). *Play: How it shapes the brain, opens the imagination, and invigorates the soul*. New York, NY: Avery.

Coyle, D., Hood, P., & Marsh, D. (2010). *CLIL: Content and language integrated learning* (Kindle Version). Cambridge, UK: Cambridge University Press.

Csikszentmihalyi, M. (1991). *Flow: The psychology of optimal experience*. New York, NY: HarperPerennial.

Eastwood, L., Coates, J., Dixon, L., & Harvey, J. (2009). *A toolkit for creative teaching in post-compulsory education*. New York, NY: McGraw-Hill International.

Edwards, B.. (1986). *Drawing on the artist within*. New York, NY: Fireside Books.

Gagnon, G. W., & Collay, M. (2001). *Designing for learning: Six elements in constructivist classrooms*. Thousand Oaks, CA: Corwin Press.

Henschke, J. A. (2009). Beginnings of the history and philosophy of andragogy 1833-2000. In V. C. X. Wang (Ed.), *Integrating adult learning and technology for effective education: Strategic approaches* (pp. 1-30). Hershey, PA: IGI Global.

Huizinga, J. (2014). *Homo Ludens Ils 86*. Abingdon, UK: Routledge. (Original work published 1949)

Jensen, E. (1998). *Teaching with the brain in mind*. Alexandria, VA: Association for Supervision and Curriculum Development.

Knowles, M. S. (1984). *Andragogy in action: Applying modern principles of adult learning*. Hoboken, NJ: Jossey-Bass.

Kolb, D. A. (1984). *Experiential learning: Experience as the source of learning and development* (Vol. 1). Englewood Cliffs, NJ: Prentice-Hall.

Kristiansen, P., & Rasmussen, R. (2014). *Building a better business using the Lego Serious Play Model*. Hoboken, NJ: Wiley.

Meir, D. (2000). *The accelerated learning handbook: A creative guide to designing and delivering faster, more effective training programs*. New York, NY: McGraw- Hill.

Merriam, S. B. (2001). Andragogy and self-directed learning: Pillars of adult learning theory. *New Directions for Adult and Continuing Education, 89*, 3-14.

Panksepp, J., & Beatty, W. W. (1980). Social deprivation and play in rats. *Behavioral and Neural Biology, 30*, 197-206.

Puccio, G. J., Mance, M., & Murdock, M. C. (2011). *Creative leadership: Skills that drive change* (2nd ed.). Thousand Oaks, CA: Sage.

Rosenzweig, M. R., Bennett, E. L., Diamond, M. C., Wu, S. Y., Slagle, R. W., & Saffran, E. (1969). Influences of environmental complexity and visual stimulation on development of occipital cortex in rats. *Brain Research, 14*(2), 427-445.

Torrance, E. P. (1979). An instructional model for enhancing incubation. *Journal of Creative Behavior, 13*(1), 23-35.

Torrance, E. P., & Safter, T. (1990). *The incubation model of teaching*. Buffalo, NY: Bearly Limited.

Von Stumm, S., Hell, B., & Chamorro-Premuzic, T. (2011). The hungry mind: Intellectual curiosity is the third pillar of academic performance. *Perspectives on Psychological Science, 6*(6), 574-588. doi:10.1177/1745691611421204

Wilson, F. R. (2010). *The hand: How its use shapes the brain, language, and human culture*. New York, NY: Random House.

About the Authors

Juliana Sánchez-Trujillo is a professor at Universidad de la Sabana in Bogota, Colombia, and a creativity and innovation consultant and trainer. Her research is focused on active learning strategies and on the development of innovative cultures. She has a Bachelor's degree in Communications, and an Master of Science in Creativity from the International Center for Studies in Creativity at SUNY Buffalo State.

Twitter: @julianacreativa
Email: juliana.sanchez1@unisabana.edu.co
Blog: destinocreativo.blogspot.com

Erica Swiatek is a passionate facilitator, consultant and trainer. She helps clients to think and lead more creatively, which helps them to be more innovative. Erica has a Master of Science in Creativity from the International Center for Studies in Creativity at SUNY Buffalo State. She loved it so much she is now an adjunct faculty member at Buffalo State.

Twitter: @ericaswiatek
Email: erica.swiatek@innovatefaster.com
Website: www.innovatefaster.com

ORGANIZATIONAL
CREATIVITY

Does a Culture of Continuous Improvement Support Creativity and Innovation?

W. Clayton Bunyard
International Center for Studies in Creativity
SUNY Buffalo State

Abstract

Continuous improvement programs, such as lean thinking and Six Sigma, have gained prominence in organizations since their introduction in the mid-1980s. These programs seek to create organizational cultures which foster continuous incremental innovations in support of efficiency, quality, and productivity. Concerns have emerged as to whether such a strong focus on incremental innovation could harm an organization's creativity and its ability to implement more radical innovations. This paper explores that concern by examining the philosophy of continuous improvement and connections in the literature of creativity and innovation. It recommends ways to strengthen the relationship between continuous improvement and creativity and explores how continuous improvement might be integrated with radical innovation.

Does a Culture of Continuous Improvement Support Creativity and Innovation?

The story of how the Post-it Note was created at 3M (Fry, 1987) is a familiar one, often told to show how the right company culture can foster breakthrough innovation. The Post-it Note is just one of a number of examples which gave 3M a strong reputation of having a creative culture which fosters innovation. Almost 20 years after the Post-it Note's introduction on the market, 3M suffered financial challenges which led to the hiring of CEO James McNerney in 2001. He pursued a range of programs to put 3M back in financial order, one of which was introducing the quality and efficiency improvement program Six Sigma (Hindo, 2007). The implementation of this highly structured, statistics-based process-improvement program (Linderman, Schroeder, Zaheer, & Choo, 2003) resulted in the significant profitability and margin improvements that followed over the next several years (Hindo, 2007).

After McNerney left 3M in 2005, new CEO George Buckley was faced with a dilemma. While the Six Sigma program enhanced efficiency and profitability, it also appeared to negatively affect creativity and innovation in research and development (Hindo, 2007). Geoff Nicholson, who is regarded as the "father" of the Post-it Note, later said "the Six Sigma process killed innovation at 3M" (Huang, 2013). In an effort to reinvigorate the company's climate for creativity, Buckley relaxed the requirements for application of Six Sigma principles in research and development at 3M (Hindo, 2007).

Nearly 10 years later, concerns persist that Six Sigma and other efficiency and quality-based continuous improvement (CI) programs could be detrimental to creativity and innovation (Ashkenas, 2012; Chen & Taylor, 2009; Suman, 2013). At the same time, proponents believe these programs can foster creativity and innovation when used appropriately (Bloomberg Businessweek, 2007; Hoerl & Gardner, 2010).

Efficiency and quality programs focus on maximizing resources, reducing risk and variability, and standardizing work practices (Chen & Taylor, 2009). These concepts make sense on the manufacturing floor, but what is their role in innovation? If a corporate culture devotes itself to continuous improvement, will it support creativity, and can it still produce radical innovations? These are questions I would like to address as a researcher in a company that has a history of innovation and has also recently begun to instill a culture of continuous improvement.

Putting Creativity and Innovation into Context

Before identifying the connections between creativity, innovation, and continuous improvement, definitions of creativity and innovation within organizations is needed to provide context. Creativity has been defined as the production of solutions that are original, elegant, and high in quality (Besemer & O'Quin, 1999; Christiaans, 2002; Ghiselin, 1963; Mumford & Gustafson, 1988; Mumford, Hester, & Robledo, 2013), and innovation has been defined as "the crafting, often reworking, of creative problem solutions into new products, processes, or services" (Mumford, Hester, & Robledo, 2013, Definitions section, para. 4).

Innovation can range in degree from incremental to radical. Incremental innovation involves small changes through the application of exploitative learning to improve existing products and processes, and can be thought of as more convergent in nature. In contrast, radical innovation results in much greater change and is based upon exploratory learning applied to new products and opportunities, and can be thought of as more divergent in nature (Damanpour & Aravind, 2013).

For organizations to thrive, they need to be able to implement both incremental and radical innovations (Damanpour & Aravind, 2013). The inherent tension of accomplishing both within an organization has long been a topic of discussion (Mumford & Hunter, 2005a). Bergqvist and Helander (2013) noted that the work on how to resolve this tension addresses it on a conceptual level, but not in the context of particular management approaches. Focusing on a more specific context—in this case CI—can provide more clarity on how it might influence the creativity and innovation capabilities of an organization.

Overview of Continuous Improvement

CI definitions have evolved over the years (Sanchez & Blanco, 2014). Dahlgaard, Khanji, and Kristensen (2008) illustrated the concept simply as "small continual changes for the better" (p. 273). Bessant, Caffyn, Gilbert, Harding, and Webb (1994) clarified CI's connection to innovation as "a company-wide process of focused and continuous incremental innovation" (p. 18). Sanchez and Blanco (2014) synthesized a number of previous definitions for CI as "the continuous process of improvement in the company done with the participation of all staff" (p. 988), which clearly delineated the level of involvement expected within an organizational culture: *all staff.* Sanchez & Blanco further noted that removing all forms of waste and finding opportunities for advancement is the primary means for improvement.

Quality and efficiency programs such as lean production, lean thinking, Six Sigma, lean Six Sigma, and Total Quality Management (TQM), have existed in one form or other in organizations since the 1980s (Sanchez & Blanco, 2014). Lean production, based on a study of the Toyota Production System (TPS) in Japan, became prevalent after publication of *The Machine That Changed the World* (Womack, Jones, & Roos, 1990). Its primary focus was eliminating waste in all aspects of production. This removal of waste allows for a continuous flow of production at reduced costs (Bhuiyan & Baghel, 2005). In the last 25 years, lean principles (now most commonly known collectively as *lean thinking* or simply *lean*) have evolved beyond the manufacturing floor and been applied to other settings (Hines, Holweg, & Rich, 2004). As such, lean should be considered as a framework with both strategic and operational levels, where the former focuses on understanding value and the latter focuses on tools for eliminating waste (Hines et al., 2004).

Six Sigma has been one of the most influential CI programs since its introduction by Motorola in 1986 (Bhuiyan & Baghel, 2005; Hoerl & Gardner, 2010). Linderman et al. (2003) described it as "an organized and systematic method for strategic process improvement and new product and service development that relies on statistical methods and the scientific method to make dramatic reductions in the customer-defined defect rates" (p. 195). Its goal of reducing unwanted variability to effectively zero can be applied to many functions of an organization (Bhuiyan & Baghel, 2005). As a complement to lean thinking, it can be practiced as the hybrid "lean Six Sigma" (Bhuiyan & Baghel, 2005).

Academic literature on CI programs has provided evidence of both the beneficial and negative consequences for employee work environments and productivity, with much of the focus on manufacturing contexts (Hasle, 2009; Hasle et al., 2012). It is difficult to draw broad conclusions about the consequences of varied approaches, as it "depends on the type of work, the design of lean, and the implementation of lean" (Hasle, 2009, p. 4). Given that evaluation depends on context—and in light of the limited literature available on the connection of any one CI methodology with creativity and innovation—this paper will look for connections across a number of CI methods.

Systematic Use of Tools Leads to Culture Change

To the casual observer, CI programs are synonymous with tools and processes. Johnstone, Pairaudeau, and Pettersson (2011) noted that "most, if not all, of the texts that have been written about lean thinking and prominent lean companies refer to an evolution from process improvement tools to a culture of continuous improvement or a 'lean philosophy' over time" (p. 53).

Finding Problems Is Encouraged

Problem solving is a critical component of CI programs. Shook (2010) articulated its importance following the study of a lean culture transformation at an automotive manufacturing plant:

> The way to change culture is not to first change how people think, but instead to start by changing how people behave—what they do.... (para. 27) The most important and difficult "cultural shift" that has to occur in a lean manufacturing transformation revolves around the entire concept of problems. What is our attitude toward them? How do we think about them? What do we do when we find them? What do we do when someone else finds and exposes one?... (para. 43) Making it easy to learn from mistakes means changing our attitude toward them. That is the lean cultural shift. (para. 47)

To support this cultural shift, employees are taught structured problem-solving methods derived from the scientific method, such as Plan-Do-Check-Act (PDCA) in lean thinking (Lander & Liker, 2007), and Define-Measure-Analyze-Improve-Control (DMAIC) in Six Sigma (Nave, 2002). These methods emphasize clarifying the root cause of a problem first, using diagnostic thinking tools such as the "5 Whys" (Johnstone et al., 2011). Once a root cause is identified, problem-solving methods can be used to prevent a recurrence of the problem.

It Takes More than Tools to Create Change

Problem-solving tools are critical to CI, but a singular focus on tools will not lead to sustained improvements and organizational change. Transformation is accomplished only if the processes and tools are integrated into a broader system for organizational culture change (Hines et al., 2004; Johnstone et al., 2011; Sony & Naik, 2012). Basadur and Robinson (1993) observed that implementation of TQM failed in organizations where a tools-only focus existed. Where it succeeded, an overarching strategy including management support, employee skill-building and engagement existed (Basadur & Robinson, 1993).

Basadur (1992) praised the CI cultures of several Japanese companies as being "better students of creativity than North Americans" (p. 29) for their higher emphasis on *finding* problems in addition to their focus on *solving and implementing* solutions to problems. These companies, operating on the belief that "workers get motivated when they get a chance to be creative on the job" (Basadur, 1992, p. 35), were also apparently able to tap intrinsic motivation to gain active employee participation. This was evinced by high numbers of submitted suggestions for improvement per employee (Basadur, 1992).

Continuous Improvement Methods Have Their Place

In response to criticisms mentioned previously (Hindo, 2007), Hoerl and Gardner (2010) argued for appropriate applications of lean and Six Sigma methods. DMAIC in Six Sigma is best applied to realize the maximum improvement possible in a defined process and in cases where the solution to the problem is unknown. It was not intended for routine problem solving. Lean approaches, they suggested, work best in situations where it is already acknowledged that a process is not working optimally, and "known solutions" can be developed to address the problems (Hoerl & Gardner, 2010). Going beyond the design of existing processes or products requires the use of development approaches such as Design for Six Sigma (DFSS) or lean product and process development (Ward & Sobek, 2014). Hoerl & Gardner went on to note that lean and Six Sigma "each cultivate and utilize creativity but are not the best approach to identifying opportunities to innovate at the business level" (p. 32) and should instead be used in combination with approaches that do.

Ruffa (2008) further cautioned the application of CI tools beyond their intended scope, particularly where there is no precedence for applicability. "It is hard to see how operational improvement techniques can be applied directly to the steps for creating new discoveries" (Ruffa, 2008, p. 202).

Development Is Not the Same as Manufacturing

When CI requires going beyond existing product or process designs, development approaches such as DFSS or lean product and process development are more appropriate (Hoerl & Gardner, 2010). In lean thinking, product and process development focuses more on the creation of value, in contrast to the manufacturing focus on eliminating waste (Ward & Sobek, 2014). That value comes from generating usable knowledge through "exploring multiple solutions simultaneously by aggressively learning about the solutions, and eliminating weak ones [and] by converging on a solution only after it has been proven" (Sobek, 2007, slide 22).

Bergqvist and Helander (2013) studied the application of lean product development in five Swedish companies to understand how to combine creativity with efficiency. In the companies that attempted to balance short- and long-term development, lean approaches focused on creating flow in product development versus eliminating waste, which is consistent with Reinertsen (2009). The companies which progressed the most in the implementation of lean product development had both support from management and lean education programs in place. In an effort to foster more efficient and timely project progress, several companies limited the number of projects per person and tried to mitigate project disturbances to allow their engineers to focus.

Bergqvist & Helander (2013) observed strong correlations between implementation of lean thinking and a decrease in slack time and skunk work. *Slack time* is the time available to people in excess of what is needed to complete their assigned work (Nohria & Gulati, 1997). *Skunk work* includes any unofficial creative work people may attempt in that excess time (Bergqvist & Helander, 2013). Slack time is analogous to Ekvall's (1996) creative climate dimension of *idea time*. While the companies did not see creativity as being incompatible with their implementations of lean, creativity was not a deliberate focus for any of the companies in the study. Bergqvist and Helander (2013) suggested that creativity was fostered by the higher levels of slack time before the implementation of lean, and that a more deliberate focus on creativity is needed in a lean culture where slack time is less available.

Continuous Learning Leads to Continuous Improvement

"A true Toyota-like organization is one that is continuously improving, constantly learning, and relentlessly learning to learn" (Lander & Liker, 2007, p. 3697). While not explicitly stated, the creation of a learning organization is the goal of CI programs (Hines et al., 2004). But does that actually happen?

Kovach and Fredendall (2013) looked at the relationship of continuous improvement practices (CIPs) with learning and organizational improvement by surveying members of a quality-focused professional organization. Increased use of CIPs did not directly support organizational improvement (i.e., performance relative to competitors), but it did result in increased learning. If the maturity of the organization's use of CIPs (or the extent to which the CIPs were incorporated in the way the company works) was considered, learning did have an impact on organizational improvement. The authors explained this mediating relationship of learning and maturity of practice as being an indication of an individual's understanding of their work environment. This understanding materialized through social participation in structured problem-solving activities. As those activities became integral to work, significant overall improvement occurred (Kovach & Fredendall, 2013).

A study of the influence of Six Sigma practices on innovation showed a similar result where organizational learning also mediated the relationship (Sony & Naik, 2012). They examined the different elements of Six Sigma practices, including Six Sigma consultants, structured improvement procedures, and use of metrics, for any influence on organizational learning and innovativeness. Their models indicated that these constructs positively related to organizational learning. The use of metrics and consultants also positively related to innovativeness, but in contrast, the structured improvement procedures had a negative impact. The authors noted that this negative interaction might substantiate the quality-creativity paradox (Sanders, 2007) in Hindo's (2007) 3M case study.

Continuous Improvement Methodologies Do Not Necessarily Foster Creativity Equally

"Creativity is undermined unintentionally every day in work environments that were established—for entirely good reasons—to maximize business imperatives such as coordination, productivity, and control" (Amabile, 1998, p. 77). Since CI programs focus on these same business imperatives (Chen & Taylor, 2009), it raises the question whether they might negatively influence the creative climate. While no formal studies examining the creative climate of CI companies have been published, two studies were identified which provide some insight into this question.

Ekvall (2000) surveyed R&D and production engineers about how CI strategies such as lean production, just-in-time, TQM, Kaizen, and ISO 9000 influenced their creative potential at work. Of those, Kaizen, a Japanese term often used interchangeably with "continuous improvement," was the most focused on problem solving, and was the most positively-viewed practice for stimulating creativity. Lean production, just-in-time, and ISO 9000, which emphasize efficiency, quality, and standardization, rated the lowest of the group. TQM was ranked between these two extremes.

A lean Six Sigma program was attributed with creating a more positive work environment in a pharmaceutical company (Johnstone et al., 2011). This was indicated by changes in employee responses over a three-year period before and after adoption of the program. Employees felt they were increasingly recognized for problem solving and innovation, and that their ideas were being actively considered (Johnstone et al., 2011).

Continuous Improvement Needs a More Deliberate Connection to Creativity

If a culture of CI supports the development of problem-solving skills, fosters an environment where individuals bring problems forward, and results in organizational learning, it inherently has a number of elements which foster creativity on an individual, group, and organizational level (Mumford & Hunter, 2005a). However, it is not apparent that those connections to creativity are deliberate. The CI literature does not clearly define its relationship with creativity in practice even though the "unleashing of employee's creativity" (De Cock, 1993, p. 156) has been acknowledged to be important to the success of CI programs (Hoerl & Gardner, 2010).

The most deliberate connection to creativity can be made with the structured problem-solving methods for generating opportunities for improvement, causes of problems, and solutions. It is difficult to determine solely from the academic literature which creativity principles and tools are applied to these methods within organizations. A limited review of some reference materials (Staudter et al., 2008), online searching, and discussions with lean thinking facilitators (personal communication, September 18, 2014) suggests that a number of creativity tools are used to promote divergent thinking (Staudter et al., 2008), with rules that are relatively consistent with established divergent thinking principles (Puccio, Mance, & Murdock, 2011). Although, the extent of application of these principles and tools across CI organizations is unclear. Based on these same resources, the appreciation for the role of creativity during selection and development of options is less evident. Staudter et al. (2008), for example, provides divergent thinking principles (Puccio et al., 2011) for brainstorming but does not provide analogous convergent thinking principles to be used with the provided evaluation tools. This is not surprising, as creativity is often mistakenly equated with divergent thinking (Robledo, Hester, Peterson, & Mumford, 2013). Research has shown that when evaluation tools based on efficiency standards were used, new technologies were less likely to be adopted than when innovation-focused standards were applied (Mumford & Hunter, 2005a). This suggests that the effectiveness of CI methods could be enhanced by incorporation of convergent thinking principles and creativity tools for evaluation and development.

Bridges Can Be Built Between Continuous Improvement and Radical Innovation

Creativity is equally important to radical innovation and to the incremental innovation that occurs within CI. Problems exist in both cases that need original, workable solutions. These different degrees of innovation support different forms of creativity (Mumford & Hunter, 2005b). If an organizational culture is focused on CI, would it hinder radical innovation? The multifaceted reasons why radical innovation is so difficult are not usually attributed to an organization's lack of ability to generate the ideas to support it (Damanpour & Aravind, 2013; Mumford & Hunter, 2005a).

When both radical and incremental innovation are desired, providing means to integrate the two is essential, particularly when developing and commercializing radical innovations (Gassmann, Widenmayer, & Zeschy, 2012). To foster this connection, Smith (1993) suggested integrating CI with creativity and innovation by thinking of it as a continuum of change to facilitate individual engagement and foster implementation of the appropriate level of change required. This continuum is based on the Kirton (1976) Adaption-Innovation model and is ordered from more adaptive to innovative: "efficiency (doing things right)", "effectiveness (doing the right things)", "cutting (doing away with things)", "improving (doing things better)", "copying (doing things other people are doing)", "different (doing things no one else is doing)" and "impossible (doing things that can't be done)" (Smith, 1993, p. 29-32).

Lean thinking may offer a means to integrate continuous improvement with radical innovation. In *The Lean Startup,* Ries (2011) presented approaches to help startup companies create disruptive innovations. These approaches are adapted from the principles of lean thinking, focusing on value creation and generation of usable knowledge (Ward & Sobek, 2014). If *The Lean Startup* approach is applied to radical innovation, its common language with lean thinking might facilitate the presence and integration of both in an organization.

Conclusion

It is clear that CI programs support organizations' ability to innovate by promoting continuous, incremental innovations. These innovations play a different and complementary role to radical innovations for driving business growth. The way organizations implement CI programs is critical to success, but there is not one correct method to accomplish this (Hasle, 2009). The limited research to date suggests that cultures of CI can be consistent with creative thinking. However, more research is needed to understand to what extent specific methodologies such as lean thinking and Six Sigma inherently influence creativity on an individual, group, and organizational level. Until that research materializes, a deliberate augmentation of CI programs (Firestien & Kumiega, 1994) with the attitudinal, behavioral, and climate factors which support creative thinking should lead to even greater impact to organizational innovation.

References

Amabile, T. M. (1998). How to kill creativity. *Harvard Business Review, 77*(5), 76-87.

Ashkenas, R. (2012, May 8). *It's time to rethink continuous improvement.* Retrieved from https://hbr.org/2012/05/its-time-to-rethink-continuous.html

Basadur, M. (1992). Managing creativity: A Japanese model. *The Executive, 6*(2), 29-42.

Basadur, M., & Robinson, S. (1993). The new creative thinking skills needed for total quality management to become fact, not just philosophy. *American Behavioral Scientist, 37*(1), 121-138.

Bergqvist, R., & Helander, M. (2013). *Applying lean approaches within product development—Enabler or disabler for combining efficiency and creativity?* (Master's thesis). Royal Institute of Technology. Retrieved from http://leanforum.se/x_jobb/2013/Bergqvist_Helander.pdf

Besemer, S. P., & O'Quin, K. (1999). Confirming the three-factor creative product analysis matrix model in an American sample. *Creativity Research Journal, 12*(4), 287-296.

Bessant, J., Caffyn, S., Gilbert, J., Harding, R., & Webb, S. (1994). Rediscovering continuous improvement. *Technovation, 14*(1), 17-29.

Bhuiyan, N., & Baghel, A. (2005). An overview of continuous improvement: From past to present. *Management Decision, 43*(5), 761-771.

Bloomberg Businessweek. (2007, July 1). *Scrutinizing Six Sigma.* Retrieved from http://www.businessweek.com/stories/2007-07-01/scrutinizing-six-sigma

Chen, H., & Taylor, R. (2009). Exploring the impact of lean management on innovation capability. In *PICMET 2009* [Proceedings of the Portland International Conference on Management of Engineering & Technology, 2009] (pp. 826-834). Portland, OR: PICMET.

Christiaans, H. H. C. M. (2002). Creativity as a design criterion. *Creativity Research Journal, 14*, 41-54.

Dahlgaard, J. J., Khanji, G. K., & Kristensen, K. (2002). *Fundamentals of total quality management: Process analysis and improvement* (2nd ed.). Cheltenham, UK: Nelson Thornes Ltd.

Damanpour, F., & Aravind, D. (2013). Organizational structure and innovation revisited: From organic to ambidextrous structure. In M. D. Mumford (Ed.), *Handbook of organizational creativity* [Kindle version]. London, UK: Academic Press.

De Cock, C. (1993). A creativity model for the analysis of continuous improvement programmes: A suggestion to make continuous improvement continuous. *Creativity and Innovation Management, 2*(3), 156-165.

Ekvall, G. (1996). Organizational climate for creativity and innovation. *European Journal of Work and Organizational Psychology, 5*(1), 105-123.

Ekvall, G. (2000). Management and organizational philosophies and practices as stimulants or blocks to creative behavior: A study of engineers. *Creativity and Innovation Management, 9*(2), 94-99.

Firestien, R. L., & Kumiega, K. J. (1994). Using a formula for creativity to yield organizational quality improvement. *National Productivity Review, 13*(4), 569-585.

Fry, A. (1987). The Post-It Note: An intrapreneurial success. *SAM Advanced Management Journal, 52*(3), 4-9.

Gassmann, O., Widenmayer, B., & Zeschy, M. (2012). Implementing radical innovation in the business: The role of transition modes in large firms. *R&D Management, 42*(2), 120-132.

Ghiselin, B. (1963). Ultimate criteria for two levels of creativity. In C. W. Taylor & F. Barron (Eds.), *Scientific creativity: Its recognition and development* (pp. 30-43). New York, NY: Wiley.

Hasle, P. (2009). Lean and the psychosocial work environment. In P. Ø. Saksvik (Ed.), *Prerequisites for healthy organizational change* (pp. 1-9). doi:10.21 74/97816080501161090101

Hasle, P., Bojesen, A., Jensen, P. L., & Bramming, P. (2012). Lean and the working environment: A review of the literature. *International Journal of Operations and Production Management, 32*(7), 829-849.

Hindo, B. (2007, June 10). *At 3M, a struggle between efficiency and creativity.* Retrieved from http://www.businessweek.com/stories/2007-06-10/at-3m-a-struggle-between-efficiency-and-creativity

Hines, P., Holweg, M., & Rich, N. (2004). Learning to evolve: A review of contemporary lean thinking. *International Journal of Operations & Production Management, 24*(10), 994-1011.

Hoerl, R., & Gardner, M. (2010). Lean Six Sigma, creativity, and innovation. *International Journal of Lean Six Sigma, 1*(1), 30-38.

Huang, R. (2013, March 14). *Six Sigma "killed" innovation in 3M.* Retrieved from http://www.zdnet.com/six-sigma-killed-innovation-in-3m-7000012593/

Johnstone, C., Pairaudeau, G., & Pettersson, J. A. (2011). Creativity, innovation and lean sigma: A controversial combination? *Drug Discovery Today, 16*(1), 50-57.

Kirton, M. (1976). Adaptors and innovators: A description and measure. *Journal of Applied Psychology, 61*(5), 622.

Kovach, J. V., & Fredendall, L. D. (2013). The influence of continuous improvement practices on learning: An empirical study. *Quality Management Journal, 20*(4), 6-20.

Lander, E., & Liker, J. K. (2007). The Toyota production system and art: Making highly customized and creative products the Toyota way. *International Journal of Production Research, 45*(16), 3681-3698.

Linderman, K., Schroeder, R., Zaheer, S., & Choo, A. (2003). Six Sigma: A goal-theoretic perspective. *Journal of Operations Management, 21*(2), 193-203.

Mumford, M. D., & Gustafson, S. B. (1988). Creativity syndrome: Integration, application, and innovation. *Psychological Bulletin, 103*, 27-43.

Mumford, M. D., Hester, K. S., & Robledo, I. C. (2013). Creativity in organizations. In M. D. Mumford (Ed.), *Handbook of organizational creativity* [Kindle version]. London, UK: Elsevier.

Mumford, M. D., & Hunter, S. T. (2005a). Innovation in organizations: A multi-level perspective on creativity. *Multi-Level Issues in Strategy and Methods, 4*, 9-73.

Mumford, M. D., & Hunter, S. T. (2005b). The creativity paradox: Sources, resolutions, and directions. *Multi-Level Issues in Strategy and Methods, 4*, 105-114.

Nave, D. (2002). How to compare Six Sigma, lean and the theory of constraints. *Quality Progress, 35*(3), 73-78.

Nohria, N., & Gulati, R. (1997). What is the optimal amount of organizational slack?: A study of the relationship between slack and innovation in multinational firms. *European Management Journal, 15*(6), 603-611.

Puccio, G. J., Mance, M., & Murdock, M. C. (2011). *Creative leadership: Skills that drive change* (2nd ed.). Thousand Oaks, CA: Sage.

Reinertsen, D. G. (2009). *The principles of product development flow: Second generation lean product development*. Redondo Beach, CA: Celeritas.

Ries, E. (2011). *The lean startup*. New York, NY: Crown.

Robledo, I. C., Hester, K. S., Peterson, J. B., & Mumford, M. D. (2013). Creativity in organizations: Conclusions. In M. D. Mumford (Ed.), *Handbook of organizational creativity* [Kindle version]. London, UK: Elsevier.

Ruffa, S. A. (2008). *Going lean: How the best companies apply lean manufacturing principles to shatter uncertainty, drive innovation, and maximize profits.* Saranac Lake, NY: Amacom.

Sanchez, L., & Blanco, B. (2014). Three decades of continuous improvement. *Total Quality Management, 25*(9), 986-1001.

Sanders, S. (2007). The quality/creativity paradox. *Quality Progress, 40*(8), 6.

Shook, J. (2010, January 1). *How to change a culture: Lessons from NUMMI.* Retrieved from http://sloanreview.mit.edu/article/how-to-change-a-culture-lessons-from-nummi/

Smith, R. C. (1993). Seven levels of change model: A process for linking creativity, innovation and continuous improvement. In S. S. Gryskiewicz (Ed.), *Discovering creativity: Proceedings of the 1992 International Creativity and Innovation Networking Conference.* Greensboro, NC: Center for Creative Leadership.

Sobek, D. K., II (2007, May 1). *Lean product and process development* [PDF document]. Retrieved from http://www.lean.org/events/webinarhome.cfm#lppd

Sony, M., & Naik, S. (2012). Six Sigma, organizational learning and innovation. *International Journal of Quality & Reliability Management, 29*(8), 915-936.

Staudter, C., Mollenhaer, J. P., Meran, R., Roenpage, O., von Hugo, C., & Hamalides, A. (2008). *Design for Six Sigma + lean toolset: Implementing innovations successfully.* (S. Lunau, Ed.). Berlin, Germany: Springer.

Suman, M. (2013, July 31). *Mike Suman: Can lean kill innovation—you be judge.* Retrieved from http://www.mlive.com/business/west-michigan/index.ssf/2013/07/mike_suman_can_lean_kill_innov.html

Ward, A. C., & Sobek, D. K., II (2014). *Lean product and process development.* Cambridge, MA: Lean Enterprise Institute.

Womack, J., Jones, D., & Roos, D. (1990). *The machine that changed the world.* New York, NY: Macmillan.

About the Author

W. Clayton Bunyard is a technical leader in corporate research at Kimberly-Clark Corporation. He has a Ph.D. in Chemistry from the University of North Carolina at Chapel Hill, and is currently a Master of Science in Creativity candidate at the International Center for Studies in Creativity and SUNY Buffalo State. His research interests center on the applied aspects of organizational creativity.

Twitter: @claybunyard
LinkedIn: https://www.linkedin.com/pub/w-clayton-bunyard-ph-d/14/388/821

Are the Other Benefits of Group Creativity Practices Just as Important as Good Ideas?

David Eyman
International Center for Studies in Creativity
SUNY Buffalo State

Abstract

This paper explores the possibility that additional benefits of group creativity processes—specifically brainstorming—might hold a value that equals or exceeds that of good ideas. This paper describes how to determine what additional outcomes of group creativity might be achieved. More specifically, it reviews six additional outcomes of brainstorming: consensus building, team building, post-session ideas, engagement, motivation, and depth of understanding. Multiple group creativity models such as Creative Problem Solving (Osborn, 1953), design thinking (Curedale, 2013), and community engagement strategy (Block, 2008) are considered in this review. Examples that support research findings are included.

Are the Other Benefits of Group Creativity Practices Just as Important as Good Ideas?

Brainstorming is a frequently misused term that has come to mean anything from a synonym for creativity to group meetings where ideas are supposed to occur but don't (Davis, 2004). Correct use of the word brainstorming would describe a facilitated divergent thinking tool following specific rules to produce new ideas that are further from the expected (Osborn, 1953). Since its birth in the early 1950s, brainstorming has come under scrutiny for efficacy in producing more or better ideas than other forms of ideation. Those who challenge brainstorming have based their opinion and research on proving or disproving efficacy in only one domain: more or better ideas.

So why do we still use brainstorming (by definition) in almost all creative thinking frameworks such as Creative Problem Solving (Osborn, 1953), design thinking (Curedale, 2013), Systematic Inventive Thinking (Boyd & Goldenberg, 2014), and Brainswarming (McCaffrey, 2014)? Some of the newer frameworks (Systematic Inventive Thinking, Brainswarming) even hide the technique under other assertions, yet still use divergence with rules, just as Brainstorming does. The most plausible explanation is that brainstorming works. And it works not only for the production of novel ideas, but for many outcomes such as team building, consensus building, and engagement (which will be discussed in depth in this paper). Additional outcomes have noteworthy value and should be considered when evaluating the effectiveness of brainstorming as a part of any larger problem-solving process. Does an intentional focus on only one output (a novel idea) benefit the group in the same way as group problem solving sessions that yield these other benefits?

What Is at Risk?

Despite debatable evidence on effectiveness (Taylor, Berry, & Block, 1958; Kohn & Smith, 2011), businesses continue to use group creativity processes with successes that transcend the original intent of generating ideas (Faure, 2004; Sutton & Hargadon, 1996). The dispute over the effectiveness of brainstorming revolves around the corporate expectation of producing big ideas desperately needed to compensate for a lack of ongoing innovation. If a big idea does not occur within one short ideation session, the blame is often assigned to the process.

More specifically, brainstorming is often blamed whether or not it is facilitated properly. Critics stereotypically judge the effectiveness of the process based on the success or failure in the production of that big idea and in so doing negate the cumulative value of the group creativity process (Sawyer, 2007; Cain, 2013).

Design thinking, as noted in Sutton and Hargadon's 1996 study of a product design firm, is an exception. In this study, design thinking yielded six important consequences: organizational memory; providing skill variety for designers; supporting an attitude of wisdom; creating a status auction; impressing clients; and providing income for the firm (Sutton & Hargadon, 1996). This study suggests that in the organizational context, idea generation deserves no special status as an effectiveness outcome.

In a lecture regarding creativity in education, Runco (2011), a noted creativity scholar and one of brainstorming's most outspoken critics, professed:

> Brainstorming does not work. Thousands of studies have been done with brainstorming, and it always lowers originality. Always. Across the board. Brainstorming is a pretty good thing...if you want team building and perhaps if you want students to exchange ideas and learn to cooperate, collaborate, and see other perspectives and so on. Those are all good things, and the brainstorming social setting might be good for it. (9:42)

In studying the collaborative effects of brainstorming on decision making, Kramer, Kuo, and Daily (1997) noted, "The use of brainstorming groups in organizations often serves multiple goals besides reaching high-quality decisions, such as team building, consensus building, or increasing participation" (p. 236).

When placing value and priority on critical factors of success such as team building, cooperation, and collaboration, we begin to appraise group creativity practices using a different measure of success than the traditional scales of quantity and quality of ideas. Sponsors of group creativity practice might be more equipped to make such decisions through an understanding of these additional outcomes.

In *Group Genius*, Sawyer (2007) wondered, "If brainstorming isn't the creativity panacea some people have thought it to be, why does its popularity persist?" (p. 66). He attributes this to an illusion of success, yet compelling evidence suggests that brainstorming's additional benefits outweigh any deficiencies in creative efficacy.

Intentions of Group Creativity

Research indicates that we claim that we want revolutionary ideas but often don't adopt them (Mueller, Melwani, & Goncalo, 2011). More frequently, we adopt small evolutionary changes to our present products, services, or ways of being. This research also supports the notion that we enter into brainstorming meetings to garner knowledge, build trust, or organize a strategic plan for achieving success. Participants and sponsors typically suggest that the intention is to generate radical innovation, yet are seldom disappointed if that objective is not met. In fact, Sutton and Hargadon (1996) reported "higher levels of satisfaction with the experience" for group brainstorming despite nominal productivity loss (p. 687). The evidence proposed that we opt for brainstorming not for creativity alone, but that group creativity sessions are superior to other meeting formats in generating other successful outcomes.

Additional Outcomes of Group Creativity

Consensus Building

With consensus, a team builds trust, confidence, accountability, and commitment to the outcome of its project. In the absence of consensus, team members may feel that their individual contributions lack value and may silently sabotage the progress by not performing to the best of their abilities, or they may move forward independently instead of as part of a cohesive team. Building consensus is critical when a project team is working toward a collaborative success, or when operating within a creative leadership model.

Group creativity processes are designed with tools and practices that lend themselves to building consensus by having every member of the team contribute in some way. In some instances, this occurs through initiating ideas and in other cases through building on others' ideas. Whether contributions are directly chosen or merged with the selected ideas, the result is that participants have added to the solution, leading to personal ownership in the outcome.

Finding consensus among group members can be challenging. For instance, people may have different problem-solving preferences (Dyer, Dyer, & Dyer, 2007; Grivas & Puccio, 2012); someone with a discovery-driven style may find it hard to agree or collaborate with someone who has an execution-driven style. And yet, the variety of cultural backgrounds, thinking styles, and even ages contributes to participants' differing opinions, which enhance creative output (Davis, 2004; Grivas & Puccio, 2012; Sawyer, 2007). Group creativity processes are ideally designed for the diversity of participants, and many group creativity tools such as Group Grids and Stakeholder Analysis (Miller, Vehar, Firestien, & Thurber, 2011) are designed to address these differences.

In a systematic group creativity session, using a methodology such as design thinking or Creative Problem Solving, selected ideas are developed by the group. The development process allocates space for further ideational thinking, which often presents further opportunities for each member to contribute. If some participants did not agree beforehand, this is often the place they can contribute the most, thereby coming to consensus with the group as the process unfolds. Compassion towards the initial idea and those who suggested it can be grown in time as the idea comes closer to a solution.

Team Building

Team building helps to foster efficient and open communication, promotes trust among employees, improves attitudes, and builds motivation toward the success of collaborative efforts. Team building is critical when the outcome of a given project is reliant on how well individual team members complement one another in a cooperative effort. Foundations of team building practices such as communication, respect, trust, compassion, support, and understanding are all enhanced by group creativity practices (Dyer, Dyer, & Dyer, 2007).

After a facilitated session, Jennifer Goodin, executive director of the Ronald McDonald House Charities of Cincinnati, noted the enhanced rapport in her group: "I'm so happy we had the entire management team in this brainstorming session. We came away from it like we're all on the same team again and working together better" (personal communication, October 27, 2014). In this session, the team balked at the hardships of implementing some ideas. Although this can be construed as a form of dissent, the team remained positive because of the directive to defer judgment. Given the need for this team's collaborative efforts and the need for iterative innovation as opposed to radically new ideas, allowing such conversations to progress within the brainstorming session helped the group in ways that a traditional team building process might not allow. Team building was the obvious outcome, benefiting the group more than radically innovative ideas.

This example echoes a research study by Henningsen and Henningsen (2013) that concluded, "Our brainstorming groups developed higher levels of cohesiveness in terms of desire to continue working with the group than nominal groups following an idea-generation task" (p. 42). The results of this study did not conclude significant idea generation gains with brainstorming, yet the additional benefits were proven significant.

Expert facilitation requires monitoring many aspects of group dynamics at once, including attending to additional outcomes of sessions. Once informed, the facilitator has the option to add more or less team building as a part of the programming, or to redirect conversations as they may support group interactions. To inspire collaborative teams, the facilitator may encourage interactions by using table teams or small-group brainstorming prior to large-group interactions. Projects may be assigned to give small groups an opportunity to witness a condensed model of their team's interaction. A post-project debrief might include discussion about the team dynamic in addition to reviewing the resulting innovations.

New Thinking and Post-Session Ideas

Creative problem solving can be enhanced by allowing a period of incubation and reflection: reflecting on the problem and gaining insights while not actively engaged in the problem. Csikszentmihalyi (1996) noted that the commercial evidence for incubation is supported in reports where after some time the creator comes to a sudden moment of insight. Participants of group sessions will emerge with ideas hours, days, even months after the session ends. At times, these late-arriving ideas are presented as refined and developed, which may support adoption. Although these ideas appear to spring from unknown sources, the depth of understanding gained in brainstorming sessions can be credited with a significant portion of new thinking.

With a knowledge base of ideas presented in sessions, a participant may also have insights into other problems he or she is presented with, and these ideas may hold value over and above the problem—solutions that were intended in the original course. The value of such ideas is situational, thereby creating a value proposition assessable only by the owner or sponsor of group creativity sessions. Gabe Tzeghai, a global innovation executive with Procter & Gamble, noted:

> The additional benefits [of group creativity] are a great source of future innovation as well. Afterward folks get ideas while driving, in the shower, on vacation, etc. Most of the ideas from the sessions don't go anywhere but the sessions can create trust that creates a broader confidence in other ideas so they may be evaluated and possibly developed into products to market. (personal communication, October 26, 2014)

Procter & Gamble has a rich history in the use of group creativity sessions and continues to employ new processes as they arise. Tzeghai observed the interrelated roles of belief, tenacity, and new product development apparent in such sessions: "Trust is the force multiplier that helps remove naysayers (aka ankle biters) and more importantly creates confidence and pace in the development of good ideas to market" (personal communication, October 26, 2014).

Engagement

Although there is some evidence of social loafing during group brainstorming sessions, there is also evidence of increased levels of project engagement emerging from sessions (Paulus, 2000; Sutton & Hargadon, 1996). Project participation, job commitment, and community engagement are all outcomes that are qualitatively evident from employees of organizations that expect creativity from employees or use group creativity methods (Gilson & Shalley, 2004).

Megan Deal, a director with People's Liberty, a philanthropic organization, has years of experience with group creativity facilitation and participation. On the topic of brainstorming, she observed:

> The results are typically team-building, eagerness, and engagement with the problem/project. I tend to subscribe to the viewpoint that participation fosters empathy and fosters understanding. When individuals are invited to contribute in early stages of brainstorming, their investment towards further stages of the project or subject matter undoubtedly balloons. (personal communication, October 23, 2014)

From this observation, it may be inferred that valuing participant input and the way they feel about participating in group brainstorming fosters future involvement with the project, job, or community. With this knowledge, engagement may become a primary objective of our initiative by shining a light on each participant's contribution. Each member's contribution builds engagement and a commitment to the outcome.

Motivation

During facilitated group creativity sessions, motivation to work on a project tends to grow (Curedale, 2013). In community engagement processes, also a modality of group creativity, this change is described as moving from a viewpoint of personal concern to a group-oriented, compassionate motivation (Block, 2008). Similarly, the design thinking approach emphasizes empathy for end users. More specifically, this approach builds optimism about empathic innovation (Curedale, 2013). Optimistic empathy-building provides motivation to direct one's efforts toward reconciling the needs of others, as well as an intrinsic motivation to succeed at innovating for the benefit of others. One possible explanation is that people are called to be responsible for successful ideation when put in the service of either end users or teammates. This redirects intent from image gain or personal expression toward solving problems on a collective level.

The use of a motivational programming structure ties together many of the additional outcomes of sessions and generates excitement toward systematic success. In *The Skilled Facilitator*, Schwarz (2005) described this possibility of some types of sessions: "In addition to clarifying survey results, these sessions are intended to create momentum and motivation for organizational change" (p. 411). By design, momentum is built into the outcome. Research by Isaksen and Gaulin (2005) affirmed that an adept facilitator is capable of maintaining motivation and group commitment during the session. Experience confirms that this continues into project motivation after the brainstorming ends.

Facilitators allow motivation to happen as a result of participants getting excited about the possibility of their ideas. The tendency is to either promote or control this energy in the room, yet there are opportune times for channeling it in ways that will balance motivation. That power will carry projects ahead at a more efficient pace and with more focus on a successful implementation.

Depth of Understanding

Group creativity promotes depth of understanding of the organization, the problem, and the individual's role in problem solving. We share critical data, build on and remember each other's ideas. We have access to multiple stores of memories and multiple ideas to build on (Brown, Tumeo, Larey, & Paulus, 1998). We ask detailed questions and nurture the collective information share. The conversation is a divergent thinking tool that builds a robust understanding of the data; then we cache pertinent details for use as needed.

At the front end of a recent problem-solving session, a group of trustees for a non-profit organization was introduced to the problem statement. The statement was carefully crafted by consultants and the president of the board. One of the trustees immediately questioned the statement and wondered why they should pursue this topic at all. The facilitators made a conscious choice to allow this comment to progress into a group discussion. The dialog appeared to have more value for the long-term health of the organization than jumping into ideation, so the group moved back into gathering data to see if the vision was worthy of exploration. On an easel pad, they listed objections. A series of questions was formed as a reaction to the complaints, and finally the group-created consensus was that not only was it worth pursuing the challenge, it was critical to do so. In the process of using this impromptu tool and allowing the conversation to unfold, each trustee gained a depth of knowledge that would never have happened outside of that meeting. Typically, this group assembles to address emergencies, report their fundraising successes, or make large decisions. The newly generated knowledge created another list of issues that will eventually need resolution and can be used to expedite all forthcoming problem-solving tasks. In some instances, this group can move to voting on issues without discussion because of knowledge gained in this session. In this particular case, the findings are self-evident, and we maintain that the depth of understanding far outweighs the original intention of the meeting.

This is valuable knowledge, so what might be done with it? For a consultant, selling problem-solving services is a vague pursuit, and the thought that we are now proposing to sell additional services muddles the pitch even further. Rather than suggest these results as by-products, perhaps these outcomes should be considered as part of the overall goals, and incorporated into the design. This might involve a deliberate selection of tools that are more conducive to one of those "additional" outcomes, or designing a new set of tools with particular goals in mind. In the above example, the tool was spontaneously created, yet it could be intentionally built into other sessions.

Conclusion

In many reviews of individual versus group creativity practice, findings might dissuade us from placing so much emphasis on group creativity or brainstorming (Cain, 2013; Dunnette, Campbell, & Jaastad, 1963; Kohn & Smith, 2011; Sawyer, 2007). Even Osborn (1953), who created (and coined the term) brainstorming, touted the merits of individual creativity: "Despite the advances in organized research, the creative power of the *individual* still counts most" (p. 289).

Even so, brainstorming in many modalities persists as the method of choice among organizations (Sawyer, 2007). There are many logical connections to explain this phenomenon, six of which are previously mentioned. We have freedom to assign our priorities to group creativity in an effort to garner the benefits that serve us best. Therefore, it is our charge to place a value on the needs of a project or team and apply the most efficient methodology that we can create. A lack of evidence indicates the need for further research to determine which group creativity tools are most efficient at creating specific, concrete results. This evidence would allow us to target specific outcomes based on our objectives.

In addition to the need for research, there is an opening for the development of tools designed to direct group creativity practice toward augmenting critical domains such as consensus, team building, late arriving ideas, engagement, motivation, and depth of understanding. This group creativity toolkit might find a comfortable home among organizational development practices; a combination of business, leadership, and creativity practices might be in order. Tying organizational development and new brainstorming tools together would support development in all areas of organizational well-being while providing a venue for new thinking.

References

Block, P. (2008). *Community: The structure of belonging.* San Francisco, CA: Berrett-Koehler.

Brown, V., Tumeo, M., Larey, T., & Paulus, P. (1998). Modeling cognitive interactions during group brainstorming. *Small Group Research, 29*(4), 495-526.

Boyd, D., & Goldenberg, J. (2014). *Inside the box: A proven system of creativity for breakthrough results.* New York, NY: Simon & Schuster.

Cain, S. (2013). *Quiet: The power of introverts in a world that can't stop talking.* New York, NY: Broadway Books.

Csikszentmihalyi, M. (1996). *Creativity: Flow and the psychology of discovery and invention.* New York, NY: HarperCollins.

Curedale, R. (2013). *Design thinking: Pocket guide.* Los Angeles, CA: Design Community College.

Davis, G. (2004). *Creativity is forever* (5th ed.). Dubuque, IA: Kendall/Hunt.

Dunnette, M. D., Campbell, J., & Jaastad, K. (1963). The effect of brainstorming effectiveness for 2 industrial samples. *Journal of Applied Psychology, 47*(1). 30-37.

Dyer, W. G., Dyer, W. G., Jr., & Dyer, J. H. (2007). *Team building: Proven strategies for improving team performance* (4th ed.). San Francisco, CA: Jossey-Bass.

Faure, C. (2004). Beyond brainstorming: Effects of different group procedures on selection of ideas and satisfaction with the process. *Journal of Creative Behavior, 38*(1), 13-34.

Gilson, L., & Shalley, C. (2004). A little creativity goes a long way: An examination of teams' engagement in creative processes. *Journal of Management, 30*(4), 453-470.

Grivas, C., & Puccio, G. J. (2012). *The innovative team: Unleashing creative potential for breakthrough results.* San Francisco, CA: Jossey-Bass.

Henningsen, D., & Henningsen, M. (2013). Generating ideas about the uses of brainstorming: Reconsidering the losses and gains of brainstorming groups relative to nominal groups. *Southern Communication Journal, 78*(1), 42-55.

Isaksen, S., & Gaulin, J. (2005). A reexamination of brainstorming research: Implications for research and practice. *Gifted Child Quarterly, 49*(4), 315-329.

Kohn, N., & Smith, S. (2011). Collaborative fixation: Effects of others' ideas on brainstorming. *Applied Cognitive Psychology, 25*(3). 359-371.

Kramer, M., Kuo, C., & Dailey, J. (1997). The impact of brainstorming techniques on subsequent group processes: Beyond generating ideas. *Small Group Research, 28*(2), 218-242.

McCaffrey, T. (2014, March 25). *Why you should stop brainstorming.* Retrieved from https://hbr.org/2014/03/why-you-should-stop-brainstorming

Miller, B., Vehar, J., Firestien, R., Thurber, S., & Nielsen, D. (2011). *Creativity unbound: An introduction to creative process* (5th ed.). Evanston, IL: FourSight.

Mueller, J., Melwani, S., & Goncalo, J. (2011). The bias against creativity: Why people desire but reject creative ideas. *Psychological Science, 23*(1), 13-17.

Osborn, A. (1953). *Applied imagination: Principles and procedures of creative thinking.* New York, NY: Scribner.

Paulus, P. (2000). Groups, teams, and creativity: The creative potential of idea-generating groups. *Applied Psychology, 49*(2), 237-262.

Runco, M. (2011, March 30). *Innovative teaching: Implications of creativity research* [Video file]. Retrieved from https://www.youtube.com/watch?v=3b9p7mBCnT4

Sawyer, R. (2007). *Group genius: The creative power of collaboration.* New York, NY: Basic Books.

Schwarz, R. (2005). *The skilled facilitator fieldbook: Tips, tools, and tested methods for consultants, facilitators, managers, trainers, and coaches.* San Francisco, CA: Jossey-Bass.

Sutton, R., & Hargadon, A. (1996). Brainstorming groups in context: Effectiveness in a product design firm. *Administrative Science Quarterly, 41*(4), 685-718.

Taylor, D. W., Berry, P. C., & Block, C. H. (1958). Does group participation when using brainstorming facilitate or inhibit creative thinking. *Administrative Science Quarterly, 3*(1), 23-47.

About the Author

As both innovation leader and industrial designer, David Eyman brings over twenty years of creative experience. As a catalyst, his expertise lies in developing new products, infrastructures, and innovation teams. His work has led to countless new products, environments, and deeper insights. David holds an Industrial Design degree from the University of Cincinnati, and is pursuing an M.S. in Creativity at the International Center for Studies in Creativity at SUNY Buffalo State.

Website: www.eymancreative.com

What Motivational Choices Might Sustain a Bottom-up Change Leader in a Large Organization?

Troy Schubert
International Center for Studies in Creativity
SUNY Buffalo State

Abstract

This paper explores the challenges faced by a bottom-up change leader working within an organization to create a work environment where creativity and innovation thrive. With an understanding that change starts from within, the author shares his personal story in grappling with long-haul motivation and resilience. He examines common barriers to connection, along with resources to extend learning for other change agents. In deconstructing leadership theory and reflecting on personal experience, he discovered a new possibility for motivation: when a change leader appreciates the simple act of human connection, a shared statement of purpose and meaning can encourage the group to persevere through change.

What Motivational Choices Might Sustain a Bottom-up Change Leader in a Large Organization?

I am a first-level manager in a large organization. Despite the fact that my role has no accountability for broad-based organizational development, I have been working to build my organization's capacity to deliver game-changing product innovations. This has been a bottom-up initiative, consistent with the nature of organizational change identified in *Deep Change: Discovering the Leader Within* (Quinn, 1996).

Remarkably, I have been relatively successful after 18 months of effort. The instrument of change has come in the form of facilitation and training in the Creative Problem Solving (CPS) process (Miller, Vehar, & Firestien, 2001; Noller, Parnes, & Biondi, 1976; Osborn, 1953; Puccio, Mance, & Murdock, 2011). More than 90 associates spread across seven innovation teams have taken part in the training. However, while I love the products that we create and develop, if it were just about product, I would have given up long ago. Championing this initiative, I have experienced the limits of my functioning capacity. In this role, I have never felt so vulnerable, exposed, and challenged—both as a practicing facilitator and as an advocate for organization-wide competency development. Nonetheless, I am compelled to overcome these barriers. One might ask: What compels me to share my passion for deliberate creativity? Considered more broadly, the question is this: In spite of the resistance that emerges in organizational change, what motivational forces might people like me, who act as change agents, tap into to sustain effectiveness and progress?

The Start of a Journey

I was introduced to CPS through SUNY Buffalo State's graduate program in Creativity. During a quiet moment after a long day on campus, I envisioned a future state in my workplace where we valued collaboration, creativity, and connection. I was moved and inspired by the vision, but given my role in the organization, I was also full of uncertainty and self-doubt. Who was I to initiate organizational change? What difference could I expect to make, given my rank and lack of seniority in the organization? I nonetheless felt called to action because I saw a need for building our capacity to think differently. Further, I saw that this could be accomplished through CPS training, an established pathway for producing such results (Puccio, Firestien, Coyle, & Masucci, 2006; Scott, Leritz, & Mumford, 2004). What I lacked in mastery of change leadership and CPS facilitation skills, I made up for with determination, tenacity, and an insatiable desire for learning. As I began to take steps toward the future that I had envisioned, I observed progress and experienced success. At the same time, I also felt the tension and resistance that exists in the gap between what we want to create and what we experience in our current reality (Fritz, 1991).

At times, I resented people who "didn't get it." Their resistance drained my energy. As a change leader, my patience waned. At times, my motivation completely dried up. If I had any hope of success, I needed to connect to a deep and sustaining source of inspiration.

A First-pass Search: Leadership and Motivation

A web search for the keywords "leadership" and "motivation" returned an abundance of resources on the topic of leadership. Fullan (2011) affirmed the appetite for such advice when he acknowledged the emergence of a multi-billion dollar enterprise built around enhancing leadership effectiveness. My cursory search addressed how to motivate others. However, several sources have validated introspection and self-awareness as powerful practices in developing and sustaining ourselves as leaders (Boyatzis & McKee, 2013; Brown, 2012; Quinn, 1996). Guided by these sources, I began to look inward for answers.

Leadership Models and Motivation

In one of the earliest models I consulted, Katz (1955) devised a leadership model grounded in technical, human, and conceptual skills. This model transcended the trait-based model of leadership (Northouse, 2012) popular at the time, because it implied that leadership could be developed like any other skill. Mumford, Zaccaro, Harding, Jacobs, and Fleishman (2000) expanded on the skills-based model, identifying motivation as one of the key individual attributes of effective leaders. Motivation, they held, is characterized by a willingness for growth and mastery, willingness to exercise influence, and a strong social commitment (Mumford et al., 2000). Reflecting on the skill sets that Katz (1995) established, motivation would most accurately be cataloged under "human" skills.

Resilient Leadership

Beyond clarity of motive, a leader also needs to develop the capacity to stay connected to their source of motivation. This goes to the heart of resilience. In other words, when motivation dries up, effective leaders find a way to get reconnected to inspiration. George (2009) characterized resilience as "a combination of heartiness, toughness and buoyancy of spirit" (p. 42). He specifically identified these leadership qualities as necessary for persevering through struggles and adversity. Reid (2008) identified resilience as a competency of successful leadership, weighed equally with skills in emotional intelligence (Goleman, 1995).

Through a deeper understanding of the skills-based leadership model, change leaders are guided to discover and clarify their sources of motivation. Further, leaders are guided to stay connected to that source of motivation and develop their capacity for resilience. A final observation is that resilience emerged as a deliberate skill employed by leaders in their quest for long-term effectiveness.

The Struggle

In developing my capacity as a change leader, I searched for the source of my motivation and worked to develop resilience. Sometimes it was there, and other times I lost sight. This was never an enjoyable experience. I wondered when the effort would pay off. Would I get promoted for this work? When would I be acknowledged for my courage and strength? Why was this so hard? How could I possibly sustain this?

Coyle (2009) studied talent development and found that high-velocity learners can be found "purposely operating at the edges of their ability" (p. 14). However, in the context of developing resilience, operating at the edges of our abilities implies we are sometimes confronted with the desire to quit. Allison-Napolitano (2014) noted, "Less resilient leaders become frenetic or withdraw in the face of disruptive change" (p. 101). While disconcerting, this observation validated the strong emotions and struggle that I experienced, including moments of self-doubt and a lack of energy to stay engaged.

Reflecting on my motivation, it was clear that I was looking externally for validation. Some colleagues did express recognition for my efforts, but I began to notice a pattern. When I received acknowledgment, I struggled to accept it. In noticing this, I had to reconsider my motives and purpose in driving this change initiative in my organization. Through self-reflection and coaching from an experienced practitioner, I began to see that my source of motivation was linked to external validation and recognition. While extrinsic motivation can be effective in propelling us into action, intrinsic motivation has been identified as a powerful attribute in catalyzing creative behaviors (Amabile, 1998; Pink, 2009a).

A Double-click on Leadership

Thus far, I have addressed leadership in broad terms, but it's useful to characterize the type of leadership I experienced through my engagement with creativity experts and change agents. To guide this exploration, I reflected on my introduction to CPS and facilitation. It was transformative, marked by a shift in personal values and self-perception. I felt empowered, appreciative, and accepting of my ability to contribute to solving problems. Cranton (1994) crystallized my experience when she defined transformative learning as the "development of revised assumptions, premises, ways of interpreting experience, or perspectives on the world by means of critical self-reflection" (p. 4).

Northouse (2012) described transformational leadership as happening when "a person engages with others and creates a connection that raises the level of motivation and morality in both the leader and the follower" (p. 186). Transformational leaders create a supportive climate, listen carefully, support followers in actualizing their potential, and treat others "in a caring and unique way" (Northouse, 2012, p. 193). Connectivity emerges as a central component in the dynamics of transformational leadership.

Connectivity is associated with innovative behavior and thriving organizational climates (Carmeli & Spreitzer, 2009), and with open, generative relationships (Dutton & Heaphy, 2003; Losada & Heaphy, 2004). Connectivity implies a safe environment for people to try new things and take risks, facilitating growth and learning through efforts in their work environment (Edmondson, 1999).

In parallel, we know that creativity practitioners work to cultivate a climate of suspended judgment, challenge, encouragement, trust, openness, playfulness, debate, and empowerment (Ekvall, 1983, 1996; Miller, Vehar, Firestien, Thurber, & Nielsen, 2011). Through comparison, we see consistency in the values and intentions of transformational leaders and creativity practitioners. Further, we become aware of connection as an element in the leader-follower relationship.

CPS Sessions Provide Insight

Through reflecting on my leadership, a new insight emerged: when I embody the core principles of CPS, I become a transformational leader working in the service of transformation for others. I create a climate of suspended judgment, trust, openness, and empowerment so that people can contribute their ideas. Their thoughts are weighed equally, regardless of origin. Through this experience, we connect in a mutual flow of give and take. This is powerfully satisfying, and made me wonder what would happen if I were motivated simply by this kind of connection. I had never considered connection as a primary motivating force.

Connection: A New Source of Motivation

When I reflected on this new, intrinsically-guided motivation for igniting change in my organization, I looked to sources that might validate this approach. Brown (2012) reflected: "Connection is why we're here. We are hardwired to connect with others; it's what gives purpose and meaning to our lives" (p. 8). This provides initial validation, but in what ways are purpose and meaning linked to motivation? Surveying four decades of motivation research, Pink (2009b) identified three foundational elements of true motivation: purpose, autonomy, and mastery. He was careful to qualify that this intrinsically-based motivation is effective in open-ended challenges where people leverage creativity (2009a). Overcoming open-ended challenges is precisely the work of change leaders. Puccio et al. (2011) identified creativity as a core competency of change leadership where novel challenges are involved. As change leaders, connection can provide meaning and purpose to our efforts and be a source of motivation in realizing visionary, novel outcomes.

The Takeaway

To reiterate the stream of logic articulated in this argument, I have deconstructed the climate that creativity practitioners work to foster and built a bridge to the principles of transformational leadership that I try to embody. Within transformational leadership, human connection emerged as a central component in leadership effectiveness. I asserted that ego-centered external motivation is unsustainable, and the possibility that human connection might be a place to focus motivation. Finally, I asserted that human connection could be a primary motivating force for sustaining my change efforts going forward.

Leaning Forward: Rebirth in Engagement and Purpose

Leading from connection is a tested pathway. Boyatzis and McKee (2013) introduced "resonant leadership," marked by strong emotional intelligence and demonstrating a "deep concern for people" (p. 4). In a compelling way, Bryant (2009) identified the link between love and leadership and asked a provocative question: "Can there really be a place for something as seemingly warm and fuzzy as love in the hard-nosed, eat-nails-for-breakfast, fear-based world of business?" (p. 10). Williamson (1992) wrote that we were born with a natural tendency to focus on love, with imaginations that are creative and flourishing. In light of that, should we sublimate an innate desire for connection when we head to the office?

We are drawn to each other, and this magnetic force is our highest purpose. Further, it is a default condition into which we are born. Subtle though it may be, the implication of this condition is that in order to build, grow, and experience connection, we need to subtract rather than add anything new; that is, we need to remove barriers to connection. As transformation begins with self-awareness, we are again guided to look inward.

Barriers to Connection

What are some of the barriers to connection? Further, how do we develop resilience in our leadership? The list below articulates some of the challenges I've encountered and offers some sources for further exploration.

Having an exit strategy. Some people are easy to connect to, and others are more difficult. If connection is our goal, then we need to seal the exit door and figure out a way to connect—even with difficult people. Brown (2012) offered several strategies to distinguish and overcome barriers to connection: practice gratitude, appreciate the beauty of cracks, set boundaries, find true comfort, and cultivate spirit.

On an uncharted path, embrace the critic. Creating something new feels like building a bridge while walking on it. What's our reaction when we realize we've made a serious mistake? How do we treat ourselves? Schwartz (2008) identified parts of our internal system that shift out of balance. The framework for his psychotherapeutic approach is outlined at his website (Schwartz, 2013).

Operating outside the comfort of conformity. Torrance (1995) urged us to "feel comfortable as a minority of one" (p. 121). This is great in theory, but when we enter the arena and long to stay connected to those we sometimes have to battle, Brown (2010, 2012) guided us to embrace our imperfection. We need to tap courage, compassion, and connection to sustain our efforts.

Wanting to quit. Few express this sentiment out loud, but engaging in a truly meaningful and challenging effort offers the opportunity to practice resilience. Petrie (2014) recommended meditation to strengthen resilience, building the muscle to bounce back from deep setbacks. Boyatzis and McKee (2013) likewise encouraged leaders to engage in deliberate renewal.

Conclusion

What would it take to awaken the desire for connection that lies dormant in all of us? What if our power to create, influence, and lead were dependent on it? In many ways, I believe that it is. Bryant (2009) stated one of the five fundamental laws of *Love Leadership*: "Fear-based leadership rules today's business landscape. But leading through fear is increasingly antiquated and self-defeating" (p. 11).

I aspire to lead from love and connection. This is a bold proclamation worthy of a life's work. To sustain myself, I will embody the spirit of transformation. Frazier (2013) eloquently stated: "To embody the spirit of a quality suggests a sense of being positively saturated with it in a way which informs not only behavior, but instills a distinct way of being, self-evident to those who witness it" (p. 77).

A Closing Story to Share

On Thanksgiving Day, I found myself putting together budgets for creativity training. Maybe it was because it was a holiday, or maybe I was simply tired, but my motivation had bottomed out. Fortunately, an e-mail crowded into my inbox:

> Today is Thanksgiving Day. I would like to take this opportunity to thank you for your great support all the time. I still remembered you arranged a great training for me, and I have learned a lot during the training. I wish you all the best, and all the best to your family! Send you a four-leaf clover: first leaf stands for hope, second leaf stands for faith, third leaf stands for love, fourth leaf stands for luck. Thanks and best regards! (Personal communication, November 27, 2014)

As change leaders, we can never know the difference we might be making. Sentiments like the note from my colleague double my resolve in continuing the change initiative in my organization. However, for the long term, we are guided to find a source of intrinsic motivation that has constancy, longevity, and power. For some, that might be love.

References

Allison-Napolitano, E. (2014). *Bounce forward: The extraordinary resilience of leadership.* Thousand Oaks, CA: Corwin.

Amabile, T. M. (1998). How to kill creativity. *Harvard Business Review*, 76(5), 76-87.

Boyatzis, R., & McKee, A. (2013). *Resonant leadership: Renewing yourself and connecting with others through mindfulness, hope, and compassion.* Boston, MA: Harvard Business Press.

Brown, B. (2010). *The gifts of imperfection: Let go of who you think you're supposed to be and embrace who you are.* Center City, MN: Hazelden.

Brown, B. (2012). *Daring greatly: How the courage to be vulnerable transforms the way we live, love, parent, and lead.* New York, NY: Gotham Books.

Bryant, J. (2009). *Love leadership: The new way to lead in a fear-based world.* San Francisco, CA: Jossey-Bass.

Carmeli, A., & Spreitzer, G. M. (2009). Trust, connectivity, and thriving: Implications for innovative behaviors at work. *Journal of Creative Behavior, 43*(3), 169-191. doi:10.1002/j.2162-6057.2009.tb01313.x

Coyle, D. (2009). *The talent code: Greatness isn't born, it's grown.* New York, NY: Bantam Books.

Cranton, P. (1994). *Understanding and promoting transformative learning: A guide for educators* (2nd ed.). San Francisco, CA: Jossey-Bass.

Dutton, J. E., & Heaphy, E. D. (2003). The power of high-quality connections. In K. S. Cameron, J. E. Dutton, & R. E. Quinn (Eds.), *Positive organizational scholarship* (pp. 263-278). San Francisco, CA: Berrett-Koehler.

Edmondson, A. (1999). Psychological safety and learning behavior in work teams. *Administrative Science Quarterly, 44*(2), 350-383.

Ekvall, G. (1983). *Climate, structure, and innovativeness of organizations: A theoretical framework and an experiment.* Stockholm, Sweden: The Swedish Council for Management and Organizational Behaviour.

Ekvall, G. (1996). Organizational climate for creativity and innovation. *European Journal of Work and Organizational Psychology, 5*(1), 105-123.

Frazier, A. (2013). What are the natural relationships between creativity and leadership? In C. Burnett & P. D. Reali (Eds.), *Big questions in creativity 2013* (pp. 69-88). Buffalo, NY: ICSC Press.

Fritz, R. (1991). *Creating.* New York, NY: Fawcett Columbine.

Fullan, M. (2011). *Change leader: Learning to do what matters most.* San Francisco, CA: Jossey-Bass.

George, B. (2009). *Seven lessons for leading in crisis.* San Francisco, CA: Jossey-Bass.

Goleman, D. (1995). *Emotional intelligence.* New York, NY: Bantam Books.

Katz, R. L. (1955). Skills of an effective administrator. *Harvard Business Review, 33*(1), 33-42.

Losada, M., & Heaphy, E. (2004). The role of positivity and connectivity in the performance of business teams: A nonlinear dynamics model. *American Behavioral Scientist, 47*(6), 740-765. doi:10.1177/0002764203260208

Miller, B., Vehar, J. R., & Firestien, R. L. (2001). *Creativity unbound: An introduction to creative process* (5th ed.). Williamsville, NY: Innovation Resources, Inc.

Miller, B., Vehar, J. R., Firestien, R. L., Thurber, S., & Nielsen, D. (2011). *Facilitation: A door to creative leadership* (4th ed.). Evanston, IL: FourSight.

Mumford, M. D., Zaccaro, S. J., Harding, F. D., Jacobs, T. O., & Fleishman, E. A. (2000). Leadership skills for a changing world: Solving complex social problems. *Leadership Quarterly, 11*(1), 11-35.

Noller, R., Parnes, S., & Biondi, A. (1976). *Creative actionbook: Revised edition of creative behavior workbook.* New York, NY: Charles Scribner's Sons.

Northouse, P. (2012). *Leadership: Theory and practice* (6th ed.). Thousand Oaks, CA: Sage.

Osborn, A. (1953). *Applied imagination: Principles and procedures of creative thinking.* New York, NY: Scribner.

Petrie, N. (2014). *Wake up: The surprising truth about what drives stress and how leaders build resilience* [White paper]. Retrieved from http://www.ccl.org/leadership/pdf/research/WakeUp.pdf

Pink, D. (2009a). *Dan Pink: The puzzle of motivation* [Video file]. Retrieved from http://www.ted.com/talks/dan_pink_on_motivation?language=en

Pink, D. (2009b). *Drive: The surprising truth about what motivates us.* New York, NY: Riverhead Books.

Puccio, G. J., Firestien, R. L., Coyle, C., & Masucci, C. (2006). A review of the effectiveness of CPS training: A focus on workplace issues. *Creativity and Innovation Management, 15*(1), 19-33. doi:10.1111/j.1467-8691.2006.00366.x

Puccio, G. J., Mance, M., & Murdock, M. C. (2011). *Creative leadership: Skills that drive change* (2nd ed.). Thousand Oaks, CA: Sage.

Quinn, R. (1996). *Deep change: Discovering the leader within.* San Francisco, CA: Jossey-Bass.

Reid, J. (2008). The resilient leader: Why EQ matters. *Ivey Business Journal, 72*(3), 1-7.

Schwartz, R. C. (2008). *You are the one you've been waiting for: Bringing courageous love to intimate relationships.* Oak Park, IL: Trailheads Publications.

Schwartz, R. C. (2013). *The internal family systems model outline.* Retrieved from http://www.selfleadership.org/outline-of-the-Internal-family-systems-model.html

Scott, G., Leritz, L. E., & Mumford, M. D. (2004). Types of creativity training: Approaches and their effectiveness. *Journal of Creative Behavior, 38*(3), 149-179. doi:10.1002/j.2162-6057.2004.tb01238.x

Torrance, E. P. (1995). *Why fly?* Norwood, NJ: Ablex.

Williamson, M. (1992). *A return to love: Reflections on the principles of a course in miracles.* New York, NY: HarperCollins.

About the Author

Troy Schubert's career has been focused on product development. His current passions include blending and bending the disciplines of product development, change leadership, facilitation, and Creative Problem Solving.

Email: tdschubert@icloud.com
Twitter: @TroySchubert

SYSTEMS of
CREATIVITY

How Does Nature Nurture Creativity?

Jennifer A. Quarrie
International Center for Studies in Creativity
SUNY Buffalo State

Abstract

The profound relationship between humans and their natural environment has been celebrated since the dawn of humanity, providing inspiration, perspective and sustenance. Neuroscience research indicates that time with nature provokes an alpha wave brain state of alert relaxation that helps humans heal significantly faster compared to exclusively man-made environments. Separate research shows that alpha waves also play a key role in creative thinking, particularly in focusing attention, suppressing sensory input to bolster internal processing, perceiving more clearly, and learning more readily. If natural physical environments that foster self-healing also nurture creativity, we can leverage time with nature as a deliberate tool for fostering creativity. By intentionally integrating nature into our physical environments and thoroughly understanding its influence on our creativity, we may enhance our lives and creatively branch out by merely returning to our roots.

How Does Nature Nurture Creativity?

While nature influences our lives in countless ways, there remains little research on the influence of physical environment on creativity. Conceptually, creativity is the generation of something that is both novel and valuable, evolved from Stein's (1953) original definition. Rhodes' (1961) person-product-process-press construct highlights the influence of environment ("press") on the other aspects of creativity, providing context for people, processes, and products.

The environment includes physical, psychological, and organizational components. Most academic discussion of creative press centers on organizational environments and social dynamics (Amabile, 1983, 1996; Vithayathawornwong, Danko, & Tolbert, 2003). However, the impact of a purer physical and sensory environment on an individual's creative function is not as well understood. Yet emerging discoveries in neuroscience, cognitive science, ecology, biology, and medicine indicate that the physical environments people choose affect conscious and unconscious aspects of health and performance (McCoy & Evans, 2002; Sternberg, 2009).

Research into how physical space fosters creativity has tended to be centered on interior design and architecture (Augustin, 2014; Kristensen, 2004; Leather, Pyrgas, Beale, & Lawrence, 1998; Puccio & Cabra, 2010; Richardson, 2014; Schweitzer, Gilpin, & Frampton, 2004; Ulrich, 2001), with an increasing emphasis on bringing elements of the outdoors indoors. Time spent in nature, one particular subset of the physical environment, facilitates healing and cognitive function (Sternberg, 2009). The implication, which is explored in this paper, is that time spent with nature likely has a direct, positive, multilateral impact on individual and group creativity, and should be utilized as a tool not only to stimulate creativity, but to live more holistic, pleasurable, and productive lives.

Why Are We Drawn to Nature?

Inspiration

Thoreau said, "It is the marriage of the soul with nature that makes the intellect fruitful, and gives birth to imagination" (1927, p. 54). Some of the greatest art, literature, and inventions have derived from witnessing, reflecting, and mimicking nature. Historically, famous creators such as Leonardo da Vinci, Ralph

Waldo Emerson, Benjamin Franklin, and Ansel Adams looked to nature for their deepest revelations. Many eminent creators held daily rituals involving walks in nature, including Russian composer Pyotr Ilyich Tchaikovsky, German pianist and composer Ludwig van Beethoven, American naturalist Charles Darwin, English poet John Milton, English author Charles Dickens, Danish philosopher Søren Kierkegaard, and German philosopher Immanuel Kant (Currey, 2013; Dunne, 2014; Grose, 2013; Nichols, 2014). During a stay along the shores of Lake Como in the Italian town of Bellagio, Franz Liszt wrote, "I feel that all the various features of Nature around me...provoked an emotional reaction in the depth of my soul, which I have tried to transcribe in music" (Csikszentmihalyi, 1996, p. 134). We can all be inspired by nature's profundity, recognize its impact, and use it in our creative work.

Perspective

The link between nature and creativity goes well beyond inspiration. Nature provides a context in its role as a physical environment and context begets meaning. As a result of the awe-inspiring context that nature provides, it is one of our richest sources of meaning. Senge, Scharmer, Jaworski, and Flowers (2004) call this idea "seeing from the whole" (p. 53). At times the scale of nature lends us perspective and reminds us of how small we are within the greater universe. This outlook is key when it comes to creative problem solving, since a higher-level view helps tough problems seem relative and less overwhelming. A global viewpoint also assists emerging patterns and relationships to become more apparent, which can contribute toward finding solutions. It also revives our awareness that we are part of something far greater than our local communities or ourselves. This level of universal connection to others and greater shared goals evokes deep intrinsic motivation to creative problem solving and perpetuates our efforts well beyond what we would otherwise do for ourselves (Pink, 2011). It conveys the message that we are not alone, nor are we the first to attempt solving such problems as many before us have paved the way (Benyus, 2009).

Further, the influence of an environment "is always dependent on the individual's perception," and this "trait x state" combination yields unique and unpredictable outcomes that are valuable for creativity (Runco & Jaeger, 2012, p. 95; Stein, 1953). "Seeing freshly starts with stopping our habitual ways of thinking and perceiving," and nature provides an excellent physical context in which to begin doing so (Senge, Scharmer, Jaworski, & Flowers, 2004, p. 29). Additionally, observing nature helps us to see things in new ways by learning more about them from micro, macro, systems, and other perspectives. Understanding nature at the systems level helps extrapolate the intricacy of the interrelationships to other unassociated systems through interdisciplinary thinking, potentially assisting to generate novel and valuable ideas. Biomimetics, the emerging field that employs this perspective, analyzes nature's elements, designs, systems and processes for the purposes of solving complex problems—which is also a primary objective of creativity (Benyus, 2009).

Biophilia, Ecology, and Restoration

Humans feel intuitively drawn to nature on a deeply emotional level, a condition known as biophilia (Wilson, 1984). Moreover, we are physically equipped to optimally function as part of the ecosystem. Ecology describes how we exist in a state of symbiosis and mutual dependence with our surroundings and other organisms (Ecology, n.d.). There are biological reasons why we feel drawn outside on sunny days, spend hours digging in the yard, and travel long distances to experience a few precious hours by the ocean or mountainside. Our strong attraction to nature has purpose; it draws us to fill some of our most critical physical and psychological deficits, which are a consequence of lives lived increasingly indoors (Kaplan & Kaplan, 1989; Louv, 2012). Our physical links to the ecosystem benefit our bodies and minds in ways that enhance creativity through healing and enhanced cognition (Sternberg, 2009).

On the Same Wavelength: Healing and Creativity

Creative Alpha Waves

To appreciate how our minds and bodies respond to our environment, it is essential to understand what is happening at the cellular level. Neuroscience research uses brain imaging and other technologies to measure brain wave activity. Alpha waves are a type of neural oscillation in the frequency range of 8-12 Hz that predominately originate from the occipital lobe of the brain during wakeful relaxation and are strongest with eyes closed (Olga, 2012).

Since the 1970s, electroencephalography (EEG) research has shown that alpha wave brain activity is correlated with creativity, particularly during those moments in which we focus attention (Carson, 2011), suppress sensory input in order to focus inward (Foxe & Snyder, 2011), and achieve clearer mental perception and learn more easily (Kaul, 2006). In this state, we more readily make associations between previously unassociated concepts and thus generate more novel concepts and solutions.

Neuroscientific studies have shown increased alpha wave activity during specific mental activities associated with creative function. Alpha waves increased their frequency and strength during the formation of novel and valuable ideas such as during creative inspiration (Martindale & Hasenfus, 1978), escalation towards insight (Kounios & Beeman, 2009; Kounios et al., 2006), and creative ideation (Fink & Benedek, 2012). Alpha wave activity also increased when focusing attention on internal thoughts (Carson, 2011) and suppressing external sensory input to allow continued internal focus (Foxe & Snyder, 2011). Further, alpha wave activity increased when confronted with unrecognizable objects, thus showing that alpha waves are a key part of responses to novelty (Vanni, Revonsuo, & Hari, 1997). Research has even become specific enough to show that alpha waves synchronize to periods of top-down processing, where thoughts begin with a general concept and become more specific, in both convergent and divergent thinking (Benedek, Bergner, Könen, Fink, & Neubauer, 2011; Jauk, Benedek, & Neubauer, 2012).

The fact that alpha wave production increases during sensory suppression may also help explain Csikszentmihalyi's (1991) theory of flow, which holds that when an individual is fully immersed, energized, and focused on an activity, the rest of the world falls away, resulting in creativity, deep enjoyment, and an altered perception of time. Both focused and softly-focused attention plays an important role in most types of creative thinking, to include all phases of CPS (Goleman, 2013). Alpha wave activity and focus also increase during meditation (Davidson et al., 2003; Kabat-Zinn, 1994).

Healing Alpha Waves

Our senses provide a constant stream of conscious and unconscious input from the physical environment, and many inputs from nature enable the body's ability to heal (Ackerman, 1991; Sternberg, 2009). A body of medical research indicates that the alpha wave brain state of alert relaxation combats stress and its destructive physiological implications, thus creating an optimal state for healing (Sternberg, 2009). For example, a study on the impact of sunlight showed that, all other variables the same, patients with rooms on the sunnier side of the hospital healed faster and were discharged an average of three days sooner than those with windows on the shadier side (Ulrich, 1984). Several other environmental and sensory inputs that appear to significantly promote healing come from nature and may show a link to the alpha wave state. For instance, the following visual inputs have been shown to promote healing: viewing nature (Cohen & Cohen, 2009; Louv, 2012); observing patterns of fractals, branching, and self-similar repeating patterns found commonly in nature (Sternberg, 2009); and taking in blue and green spectra (the primary spectra for sky, water, and vegetation in nature) for calming (Alter, 2013; Sternberg, 2009).

Immersing in a natural environment in a active or passive way also brings healing benefits, to include such behaviors as exposure to full spectrum sunlight, preferably facing east for higher light intensity (Heschong et al., 1999; Sternberg, 2009; Ulrich, 1984); passive time in garden and forest settings (Corazon, Stigsdotter, Moeller, & Rasmussen, 2012; Li et al., 2006; Ottosson & Grahn, 2005; Simons, Simons, McCallum, & Friedlander, 2006); resting and waking in a way that allows the body clock to align with daily and seasonal circadian rhythms (Cohen & Cohen, 2009; Shiller, 2014); listening to repetitive nature sounds; smelling scents such as lavender, chamomile, geranium, rose, sweet marjoram, and valerian (Sternberg, 2009); or even handling smooth stones or beads (Montagu, 1986). Combining these elements may provide added benefit; for example, waking according to one's own body rhythm and taking in the full spectrum sunlight of the morning while gazing on a lovely natural vista (Cohen & Cohen, 2009). Further, given the stomach's role as our "second brain," the role of nature in our daily nutrition (particularly plants) is another crucial way of bringing nature in as a means to healing (Fuhrman, 2014).

Simultaneous States

Could it be that the very physical environments and sensory input that place the human body into a self-healing state also place it into an ideal state for creative thinking? The nature-inspired alpha wave brain state of alert relaxation that enables the body to direct resources towards healing may simultaneously nurture creativity and problem solving. Healing and creativity share common elements. Both promote internally-driven change in the service of improvement and adaption. They are significantly enhanced by time with nature, are improved via specific processes, require focused energy and investment, center on growth, and involve a connection between body and mind. Healing and creativity are also both paths to self-actualization (Maslow, 1943).

Based on the above, I believe that by moderating our environment, we have the power to influence and improve our own creative function. One might wonder whether habitual creative thinking can invite the alpha wave state and therein induce similar healing effects? Could those who are mentally ill and drawn heavily to creative pursuits in effect be self-medicating by inviting the alpha wave state, lowering cortisol levels and achieving the mental clarity and healing that comes with creative activity? Perhaps widely publicizing creativity's links with nature, healing, and positive psychology may also counter lingering prejudices of an exclusive causal relationship between mental illness and exceptional creativity.

Natural Environments, Creative Tools

How might we leverage the physical environment to nurture our creative functions? Restoring the natural influence in our lives in a deliberate and personalized way not only empowers us as individuals but may also expand our awareness of interconnectedness with our greater society and ecosystem and inspire us to act as creative leaders.

Creative Problem Solving (CPS)

Physical environment plays a key role in every stage of CPS, from exploring the vision to formulating an action plan (Puccio, Mance, Switalski, & Reali, 2012). The Storyboarding tool helps to develop a vision by constructing a detailed physical context that assists in developing the ideal future state, as well as considering environmental influences and helping to identify and remove constraints. Considering the environment while gathering key data and assessing the situation can cast an issue in a new and useful light. Physical environment figures prominently in the Excursions tool, during which one literally uses the physical environment to experience a novel perspective and to prompt fresh reflections on the challenge at hand (Miller, Vehar, Firestien, Thurber, & Neilsen, 2011). The Excursions tool also facilitates relaxation and reduces the amount of immediate sensory stimuli that may distract from deeper thinking. Group work, including CPS, is also impacted by the surrounding physical environment as noted in Schwarz's (2002) Group Effectiveness Model, which lists physical environment as a key element of group context (p. 19).

A natural physical environment that prompts positive emotions can also provide a stimulating yet calming setting for incubation as creators step away from deliberate thinking to allow for periodic defocused and subconscious mental processing. "When persons with prepared minds find themselves in beautiful settings, they are more likely to find new connections among ideas, new perspectives on issues" (Csikszentmihalyi, 1996, p. 136). Anecdotally, when identifying environments in which the best and most creative ideas arise, people most commonly list places like the shower, walks with the dog, or exercising outside. This echoes the daily rituals of the great thinkers, discussed earlier, who took long walks as their primary way of facilitating their personal creativity. The practice of incubation, particularly in a non-judging context such as nature, may also strengthen self-confidence in personal intuition as a complement to cognitive and affective decision-making skills (Francisco & Burnett, 2008).

Variable attention—the ability to readily switch between attention levels where attention is defocused on highly ambiguous tasks and focused on unambiguous tasks—is associated with creative people (Vartanian, 2009). Time in nature may help develop one's variable attention, as the environment demands periodic acute attention to avoid injury yet facilitates a more relaxed state the rest of the time. Poetically, Frost (1921) uses the experience of nature to mirror de Bono's (1970) theory of lateral thinking, the need to jump from our worn paths, when he encourages following the road not taken. More currently, other processes such as design thinking and biomimicry also leverage physical environment. Design thinking includes extensive field observation and empathic immersion in the users' experiences (d.school, 2014). Biomimicry also takes an acute observational approach (Benyus, 2009).

Essential Elements

Interacting with nature directly offers the greatest benefit. Gandhi once said, "To forget how to dig the earth and tend the soil is to forget ourselves" (Gandhi & Attenborough, 1982, p. 5). Yet people have long worked to extract themselves from the dangers, discomforts, and hardships of nature. Indoor environments increase our safety and comfort, while affording the luxury of spending our limited resources on more creative and cognitive pursuits. It is challenging to think divergently when preoccupied with immediate survival; say, when running from a predator, finding food, or constructing shelter. For those without much opportunity to go outside, there are ways to enjoy some benefits of experiencing nature without immersing oneself in it. Studies show that simple interactions such as watering houseplants, interacting with a pet, or even looking at a nature scene, have positive effects on stress attention levels (Kaplan & Kaplan, 1989; Sop Shin, 2007; Ulrich, 2002).

How Nature Can Nurture Creativity

Climate and Cognitive Skills

The majority of currently-popular creative methods are essentially considered to be cognitively-based, despite also having robust affective and intuitive attributes. Physical climate impacts the cognitive skills of creativity on multiple levels, to include learning, memory, awareness, mindfulness, intuition, and intention. By deliberately incorporating physical climate into our creative approach, "we seek the gifts of nature essential for the realization of our full intellectual and spiritual potential" (Louv, 2012, p. 38).

Learning, Memory and Associative Thinking

In education, the "loose parts theory" holds there is a positive relationship between the number of loose parts in an environment and the creativity of play that occurs there (Nicholson, 1971, p. 30). Nature has an almost infinite set of loose parts, particularly in comparison to any man-made environment, and may result in more creative play (Nicholson, 1971, p. 31), and also may "encourage a greater sensitivity to patterns that underlie all experience" (Louv, 2012, p. 34), thus providing the building blocks for future non-obvious associations which drive much of creativity. Some approaches to childhood education, such as Reggio Emilia and nature preschools in Scandinavia, base their learning approach on the concepts that the physical environment is "the third educator after the teacher and parent" according to Susan Lyon, executive director of the Innovative Teacher Project (Garrett, 2013, p. 1; Project Wild Thing, 2014). In them, education is based on interrelationships, and real-life experiences allow deeper questioning and theory development (Garrett, 2013; White, 2007).

The richness of the natural environment also sharpens an observer's powers of perception. Compared to more sterile indoor environments, learners absorb more information somatically, auditorily, visually, as well as intellectually, leading to a much richer understanding (Meier, 2000, pp. 42-50). Being in nature's boundless set of stimuli increases the number of associations an observer is able to make between previously unrelated objects or concepts, thus increasing the potential volume and novelty of ideas (Ulrich, 1993). Additionally, studies indicated that interaction with nature significantly improved memory and attention spans (Berman, Jonides, & Kaplan, 2008; Louv, 2012) and reduced children's Attention-Deficit Disorder symptoms (Taylor, Kuo, & Sullivan, 2001).

Awareness, Mindfulness, and Intuition

The dynamism of nature encourages awareness and mindfulness by rewarding simple observation. By remaining both aware and accepting of our observations, we extend our mental boundaries and open a path to insight. As Rodin said, "To any artist worthy of the name, all in nature is beautiful, because his eyes, fearlessly accepting all external truth, read there, as in an open book, all the inner truth" (Rodin, 1983, p. 20).

Visual thinking tools, which use imagery in various ways, are critical for creative thinking, so much so that the word "imagination" is nearly a synonym for creativity (Davis, 1999, p. 133). However, many of the studies linking imagery with creativity address only mental imagery (thought images, eidetic images, synesthesia, hallucination, dream image, and hypnopompic images) without emphasizing the utility of rich, external imagery (Davis, 1999, p. 133-135). Using nature images as part of the Forced Connections tool provides a powerful prompt for new associations (Miller et al., 2011).

Further, time in nature appears to heighten awareness and awaken more latent senses, thus improving intuition, according to a study of U.S. Marines by the Pentagon-based Joint Improvised Explosive Device Defeat Organization, which supports pre-deployment training (Perry, 2009). More importantly, this awareness extends as much internally toward observing and understanding the self as it does externally to physical surroundings.

Living Deliberately

> I went to the woods because I wished to live deliberately, to front only the essential facts of life. And see if I could not learn what it had to teach and not, when I came to die, discover that I had not lived. (Thoreau, 1854, p. 143)

Deliberately including both nature and creative-thinking habits into daily life increases the likelihood that they will become integral approaches to living fully and holistically. Time in nature may also increase the propensity for deliberate everyday creativity as personal needs arise and individuals work to fulfill them with limited available resources. Habitually spending time in nature may also develop new skill-related knowledge relative to that domain. It is therefore possible that by deliberately spending time with nature, one may increase all three primary psychological components required for creativity: motivation, the ability to make new connections, and skill-related knowledge (Runco & Richards, 1997, p. 234).

Freedom

A common feeling associated with nature is one of freedom. Nature's grand scale can promote a sense of spatial freedom away from the constraint of limited indoor spaces. Further, many are intuitively drawn to explore nature, seeking new locations of solitude or beauty, or particular resources such as certain types of water, plants, or minerals. The freedom of physical movement is an inherent part of natural exploration, not only in regard to moving one's body instead of sitting still, but also the freedom to move throughout the environment in uncharted and non-prescribed ways. Studies have suggested a direct relationship between general physical movement and increased creativity (Berger & Owen, 1988; Green, 1993; Hug, Hartig, Hansmann, Seeland, & Hornung, 2009; Rath, 2013). What's more, "green exercise is like exercised squared"; research has shown that physical movement within a natural environment has far more mental and physical health benefits than indoors on a machine (Selhub & Logan, 2012, p. 116).

Beyond the realm of the physical, nature is free of social judgment, constraint, pressure, and directive; offering a pleasant forum for solitude, concentration, rebellion, or vacation. As a result of spending time without perceived social judgment, one might reduce self-censorship and permit broader and more creative thinking, a key element to successful creative idea generation (Puccio et al., 2012).

Presence

Nature exists in the present; energy is channeled into the current circumstance and the surrounding ecosystem. Those who spend time in the ever-changing environment of nature join their ecosystem by living in the present and paying closer attention to the moment. As a result of spending time with nature, individuals may increase intuitive and mindfulness skills, which are key throughout CPS for identifying needs, understanding priorities, and assessing situations (Francisco & Burnett, 2008; Puccio, Mance, & Murdock, 2011). Presence, living in the moment, is also a key part of positive psychology, notably Csikszentmihalyi's (1997) theory of flow in everyday life, a driver of creativity and problem solving.

Social Impact

While time in nature, particularly for creative pursuits, tends to be associated with solitude, nature also significantly affects social dynamics. Just as we are built to be part of our ecosystems physically, we are also built to be social beings, part of a "mental ecosystem" with others, where we contribute our thoughts to enhance the greater thinking. Jung, for instance, wrote extensively on the collective unconscious and the idea that "part of the psyche was shared by all people, in all cultures, throughout the ages" (Jones, 1999, p. 112).

Practicing non-judgment while in nature also prepares one to maintain that perspective moving forward, continuing to offer compassion and empathy to oneself and others. While empathy is important to problem solving, it is also useful in problem finding: "Empathy with oneself is a means for perceiving inner conflicts and tensions that make good problems" (Runco, 1994, p. 106). Lowering stress hormones changes behaviors and changes one's focus, and as a result individuals in groups may behave more supportively (Sapolsky, 1994). The outdoors has also been identified as an ideal context in which children can maximize socio-cultural learning, create meaning, and learn values, such as: recognition of the equal worth of all humans, equality between the sexes, solidarity, respect for life, tolerance, justice, truth, and honesty (Aasen, Grindheim, & Waters, 2009).

Adaption

Nature offers the ultimate model for embracing change. As H. G. Wells (1945) famously noted, "Adapt or perish, now as ever, is nature's inexorable imperative." Living with this mentality may help the mind become more expectant and accepting of change, and even more responsive to it. Given creativity's role in leading and adapting to change (Puccio et al., 2012), nature not only provides a useful model but also a dynamic partner. As Johann Wolfgang von Goethe noted, "Nature knows no pause in progress and development, and attaches her curse on all inaction" (Holdrege, 2013).

Conclusion

Humans are intuitively drawn towards nature and the need for this interaction has been recognized for centuries across the globe. It is valuable to understand why humans gravitate towards nature for re-centering, creative thinking, problem solving, and healing, as well as why nature works so incredibly well to bring our best thoughts forward. While there is much yet undiscovered, our current knowledge of human-nature dynamics might just be enough to inspire significant changes in the way we choose our physical environments to create lives that deliberately nurture creativity and well-being. As we envision the future and search for the answers to tomorrow's challenges, it is time that the field of creativity focus on what our physical environment might contribute, and highlight the particular benefits that nature brings to nurture creativity.

References

Aasen, W., Grindheim, L. T., & Waters, J. (2009). The outdoor environment as a site for children's participation, meaning-making and democratic learning: Examples from Norwegian kindergartens. *Education 3-13, 37*(1), 5-13.

Ackerman, D. (1991). *A natural history of the senses.* New York, NY: Vintage.

Alter, A. (2013). *Drunk tank pink: And other unexpected forces that shape how we think, feel, and behave.* New York, NY: Penguin Press.

Amabile, T. M. (1983). The social psychology of creativity: A componential conceptualization. *Journal of Personality and Social Psychology, 45*(2), 357-377.

Amabile, T. M. (1996, January). *Creativity and innovation in organizations* [Background note]. Cambridge, MA: Harvard Business School.

Augustin, S. (2014, October 28). *Rules for designing an engaging workplace.* Retrieved from https://hbr.org/2014/10/rules-for-designing-an-engaging-workplace

Benedek, M., Bergner, S., Könen, T., Fink, A., & Neubauer, A. C. (2011). EEG alpha synchronization is related to top-down processing in convergent and divergent thinking. *Neuropsychologia, 49*(12), 3505-3511. doi: 10.1016/j. neuropsychologia.2011.09.004

Benyus, J. (2009, July). *Janine Benyus: Biomimicry in action* [Video file]. Retrieved from http://www.ted.com/talks/janine_benyus_biomimicry_ in_action#t-248039

Berger, B. G., & Owen, D. R. (1988). Stress reduction and mood enhancement in four exercise modes: Swimming, body conditioning, hatha yoga, and fencing. *Research Quarterly for Exercise and Sport, 59*(2), 148-159.

Berman, M. G., Jonides, J., & Kaplan, S. (2008). The cognitive benefits of interacting with nature. *Psychological Science, 19*(12), 1207-1212.

Carson, S. (2011). The unleashed mind. *Scientific American Mind, 22*(2), 22-29.

Cohen, M., (Producer and Director) (2009). *The Science of Healing: With Esther Sternberg* [DVD]. United States: Resolution Pictures.

Corazon, S. S., Stigsdotter, U. K., Moeller, M. S., & Rasmussen, S. M. (2012). Nature as therapist: Integrating permaculture with mindfulness-and acceptance-based therapy in the Danish Healing Forest Garden Nacadia. *European Journal of Psychotherapy & Counselling, 14*(4), 335-347.

Csikszentmihalyi, M. (1991). *Flow: The psychology of optimal experience.* New York, NY: HarperPerennial.

Csikszentmihalyi, M. (1996). *Creativity: Flow and the psychology of discovery and invention.* New York, NY: HarperCollins.

Csikszentmihalyi, M. (1997). *Finding flow: The psychology of engagement with everyday life.* New York, NY: Basic Books.

Currey, M. (Ed.). (2013). *Daily rituals: How artists work.* New York, NY: Random House.

d.school. (2014). *Method: What? How? Why?* Retrieved from http://dschool. stanford.edu/wp-content/themes/dschool/method-cards/what-why-how.pdf

Davidson, R. J., Kabat-Zinn, J., Schumacher, J., Rosenkranz, M., Muller, D., Santorelli, S. F., Urbanowski, F., Harrington, A., Bonus, K., & Sheridan, J. F. (2003). Alterations in brain and immune function produced by mindfulness meditation. *Psychosomatic Medicine, 65*(4), 564-570.

Davis, G. A. (1998). *Creativity is forever.* Dubuque, IA: Kendall Hunt.

de Bono, E. (1970). *Lateral thinking: Creativity step by step.* New York, NY: Harper Perennial.

Dunne, C. (2014, July 10). *The daily routines of 26 of history's most creative minds.* Retrieved from http://www.fastcodesign.com/3032874/infographic-of-the-day/the-daily-routines-of-26-of-historys-most-creative-minds

Ecology (n.d.). In *Encyclopædia Britannica.* Retrieved from http://www.britannica.com/EBchecked/topic/178273/ecology

Fink, A., & Benedek, M. (2012). EEG alpha power and creative ideation. *Neuroscience & Biobehavioral Reviews, 44,* 111-123. doi: 10.1016/j.neubiorev.2012.12.002

Foxe, J. J., & Snyder, A. C. (2011). The role of alpha-band brain oscillations as a sensory suppression mechanism during selective attention. *Frontiers in Psychology, 2,* 154. doi: 10.3389/fpsyg.2011.00154

Francisco, J. M., & Burnett, C. A. (2008). Deliberate intuition: Giving intuitive insights their rightful place in the creative problem solving thinking skills model. In G. J. Puccio, C. Burnett, J. F. Cabra, J. M. Fox, S. Keller-Mathers, M. C. Murdock, & J. A. Yudess (Eds.), *Proceedings from An International Conference on Creativity and Innovation Management—The 2nd Community Meeting* (Vol. 2) (pp. 164-175). Buffalo, NY: International Center for Studies in Creativity, Buffalo State.

Frost, R. (1921). *Mountain interval.* New York, NY: Henry Holt.

Fuhrman, J. (2014). *The end of dieting.* New York, NY: HarperCollins.

Gandhi, M. & Attenborough, R. (1982). *The words of Gandhi.* New York, NY: Newmarket Press.

Garrett, R. (2013, July 15). *What is Reggio Emilia?* Retrieved from http://www.education.com/magazine/article/Reggio_Emilia/

Goleman, D. (2013). *Focus: The hidden driver of excellence.* London, UK: Bloomsbury.

Green, J. (1993). *Fostering creativity through movement and body awareness practices: A postpositivist investigation into the relationship between somatics and the creative process* [Doctoral dissertation]. Retrieved from https://etd.ohiolink.edu/rws_etd/document/get/osu1226597858/inline

Grose, J. (2013, May 20). *From Beethoven to Woody Allen—The daily rituals of the world's most creative people and what you can learn from them.* Retrieved from http://www.fastcocreate.com/1682913/from-beethoven-to-woody-allen-the-daily-rituals-of-the-worlds-most-creative-people-and-what-

Heschong, L., Mahone, D., Kuttaiah, K., Stone, N., Chappell, C., & McHugh, J. (1999). *Daylighting in schools: An investigation into the relationship between daylighting and human performance* [Report]. California: Pacific

Gas and Electric Company. Retrieved from http://h-m-g.com/downloads/Daylighting/schoolc.pdf

Holdrege, C. (2014, Spring). *Goethe and the evolution of science.* Retrieved from http://www.natureinstitute.org/pub/ic/ic31/goethe.pdf

Hug, S. M., Hartig, T., Hansmann, R., Seeland, K., & Hornung, R. (2009). Restorative qualities of indoor and outdoor exercise settings as predictors of exercise frequency. *Health & Place, 15*(4), 971-980.

Jauk, E., Benedek, M., & Neubauer, A. C. (2012). Tackling creativity at its roots: Evidence for different patterns of EEG alpha activity related to convergent and divergent modes of task processing. *International Journal of Psychophysiology, 84*(2), 219-225. doi: 10.1016/j.1016/j.ijpsycho.2012.02.012

Jones, K. (1999). Jungian theory. In M. A. Runco & S. R. Pritzker (Eds.), *Encyclopedia of creativity* (Vol. 2). San Diego, CA: Academic Press.

Kabat-Zinn, J. (1994). *Wherever you go, there you are: Mindfulness meditation in everyday life.* New York, NY: Hyperion.

Kaplan, R., & Kaplan, S. (1989). *The experience of nature: A psychological perspective.* New York, NY: Cambridge University Press.

Kaul, P. (2006). Brain wave interactive learning where multimedia and neuroscience converge. In K. Elleithy, T. Sobh, A. Mahmood, M. Iskander, & M. A. Karim (Eds.), *Advances in Computer, Information, and Systems Sciences, and Engineering* (pp. 351-357). Netherlands: Springer.

Kounios, J., & Beeman, M. (2009). The aha! moment: The cognitive neuroscience of insight. *Current Directions in Psychological Science, 18*(4), 210-216. doi: 10.1111/j.1467-8721.2009.01638.x

Kounios, J., Frymiare, J. L., Bowden, E. M., Fleck, J. I., Subramaniam, K., Parrish, T. B., & Jung-Beeman, M. (2006). The prepared mind: Neural activity prior to problem presentation predicts subsequent solution by sudden insight. *Psychological Science, 17*(10), 882-890. doi: 10.1111/j.1467-9280.2006.01798.x

Kristensen, T. (2004). The physical context of creativity. *Creativity and Innovation Management, 13*(2), 89-96. doi: 10.1111/j.0963-1690.2004.00297.x

Leather, P., Pyrgas, M., Beale, D., & Lawrence, C. (1998). Windows in the workplace: Sunlight, view, and occupational stress. *Environment and Behavior, 30*(6), 739-762.

Li, Q., Morimoto, K., Nakadai, A., Inagaki, H., Katsumata, M., Shimizu, T., & Kawada, T. (2006). Forest bathing enhances human natural killer activity and expression of anti-cancer proteins. *International Journal of Immunopathology and Pharmacology, 20*(2 Suppl. 2), 3-8.

Louv, R. (2012). *The nature principle: Human restoration and the end of nature-deficit disorder.* Chapel Hill, NC: Algonquin Books.

Martindale, C., & Hasenfus, N. (1978). EEG differences as a function of creativity, stage of the creative process, and effort to be original. *Biological Psychology, 6*(3), 157-167.

Maslow, A. H. (1943). *A theory of human motivation.* Radford, VA: Wilder.

McCoy, J. M., & Evans, G. W. (2002). The potential role of the physical environment in fostering creativity. *Creativity Research Journal, 14*(3-4), 409-426. doi: 10.1207/S15326934CRJ1434_11

Meier, D. (2000). *The accelerated learning handbook.* New York, NY: McGraw-Hill.

Miller, B., Vehar, J., Firestien, R., Thurber, S., & Neilsen, D. (2011). *Creativity unbound: An introduction to creative process.* Evanston, IL: FourSight.

Montagu, A. (1986). *Touching: The human significance of the skin.* New York, NY: Harper & Row.

Nichols, W. J. (2014). *Blue mind: The surprising science that shows how being in, on or under water can make you happier, healthier, more connected and better at what you do.* New York, NY: Little, Brown.

Nicholson, S. (1971). The theory of loose parts: How not to cheat children. *Landscape Architecture, 62*(1), 30-34.

Olga, B. (2012). Comments for current interpretation EEG alpha activity: A review and analysis. *Journal of Behavioral and Brain Science, 2,* 239-248.

Ottosson, J., & Grahn, P. (2005). A comparison of leisure time spent in a garden with leisure time spent indoors: On measures of restoration in residents in geriatric care. *Landscape Research, 30*(1), 23-55.

Perry, T. (2009, October 28). *Some troops have a sixth sense for bombs.* Retrieved from http://articles.latimes.com/2009/oct/28/world/fg-bombs-vision28

Pink, D. H. (2011). *Drive: The surprising truth about what motivates us.* New York, NY: Riverhead Books.

Project Wild Thing (2014, November). *Project Wild Thing.* Retrieved from http://projectwildthing.com

Puccio, G. J., & Cabra, J. F. (2010). Organizational creativity. In J. C. Kaufman & R. J. Sternberg (Eds.), *The Cambridge handbook of creativity* (pp. 145-173). New York, NY: Cambridge University Press.

Puccio, G. J., Mance, M., & Murdock, M. C. (2011). *Creative leadership: Skills that drive change* (2nd ed.). Thousand Oaks, CA: Sage.

Puccio, G. J., Mance, M., Switalski, L. B., & Reali, P. D. (2012). *Creativity rising: Creative thinking and creative problem solving in the 21st century.* Buffalo, NY: ICSC Press.

Rath, T. (2013). *Eat move sleep: How small choices lead to big changes.* New York, NY: Missionday.

Rhodes, M. (1961). An analysis of creativity. *Phi Delta Kappan, 42,* 305-310.

Richardson, L. (2014, November 2). Fun, creativity at work gets the job done. *The Indianapolis Star.* Retrieved from http://www.indystar.com/story/money/2014/11/02/fun-creativity-work-gets-job-done/18268661/

Rodin, A. (1983). *Rodin on art and artists.* Mineola, NY: Dover Publications.

Runco, M. (1994). *Problem finding, problem solving, and creativity.* Norwood, NJ: Alex Publishing.

Runco, M. A., & Jaeger, G. J. (2012). The standard definition of creativity. *Creativity Research Journal, 24*(1), 92-96.

Runco, M. A., & Richards, R. (Eds.) (1997). *Eminent creativity, everyday creativity, and health.* Santa Barbara, CA: Greenwood Publishing Group.

Sapolsky, R. M. (1998). *Why zebras don't get ulcers: An updated guide to stress, stress-related diseases, and coping.* New York, NY: W. H. Freeman.

Schweitzer, M., Gilpin, L., & Frampton, S. (2004). Healing spaces: Elements of environmental design that make an impact on health. *Journal of Alternative and Complementary Medicine, 10*(Suppl. 1), S71-S83.

Selhub, E. M., & Logan, A. C. (2012). *Your brain on nature.* Mississauga, Canada: John Wiley and Sons Canada.

Senge, P., Scharmer, C. O., Jaworski, J., & Flowers, B. S. (2004). *Presence: Human purpose and the field of the future.* New York, NY: Random House.

Shiller, B. (2014, November 13). *Listening to your body clock can make you more productive and improve your well-being.* Retrieved from http://www.fastcoexist.com/3038029/how-listening-to-our-body-clocks-can-improve-productivity-and-raise-wellbeing

Simons, L. A., Simons, J., McCallum, J., & Friedlander, Y. (2006). Lifestyle factors and risk of dementia: Dubbo study of the elderly. *Medical Journal of Australia, 184*(2), 68.

Sop Shin, W. (2007). The influence of forest view through a window on job satisfaction and job stress. *Scandinavian Journal of Forest Research, 22*(3), 248-253.

Stein, M. I. (1953). Creativity and culture. *Journal of Psychology, 36*, 311–322.

Sternberg, E. M. (2009). *Healing spaces: The science of place and well-being.* Cambridge, MA: Belknap Press of Harvard University Press.

Taylor, A. F., Kuo, F. E., & Sullivan, W. C. (2001). Coping with ADD: The surprising connection to green play settings. *Environment and Behavior, 33*(1), 54-77.

Thoreau, H. D. (1854). *Walden* (Vol. 1). Boston, MA: Houghton Mifflin.

Thoreau, H. D. (1927). *The heart of Thoreau's journals* (O. Shepard, Ed.). Boston, MA: Houghton Mifflin.

Ulrich, R. S. (1984). View through a window may influence recovery from surgery. *Science, 224*, 420-421.

Ulrich, R. S. (1993). Biophilia, biophobia, and natural landscapes. In S. R. Kellert & E. O. Wilson (Eds.), *The biophilia hypothesis* (pp. 73-137). Washington, DC: Island Press.

Ulrich, R. S. (2001). Effects of healthcare environmental design on medical outcomes. In A. Dilani (Ed.), *Design and health: Proceedings of the Second International Conference on Health and Design* (pp. 49-59). Stockholm, Sweden: Svensk Byggtjanst.

Ulrich, R. S. (2002, April). Health benefits of gardens in hospitals. Paper presented at Haarlemmermeer, Netherlands. Retrieved from http://plantsolutions. com/documents/HealthSettingsUlrich.pdf

Vanni, S., Revonsuo, A., & Hari, R. (1997). Modulation of the parieto-occipital alpha rhythm during object detection. *The Journal of Neuroscience, 17*(18), 7141-7147.

Vartanian, O. (2009). Variable attention facilitates creative problem solving. *Psychology of Aesthetics, Creativity, and the Arts, 3*(1), 57.

Vithayathawornwong, S., Danko, S., & Tolbert, P. (2003). The role of the physical environment in supporting organizational creativity. *Journal of Interior Design, 29*(1-2), 1-16.

Wells, H. G. (1945). *Mind at the end of its tether.* London, UK: W. Heinemann.

White, J. (2007). *Being, playing and learning outdoors: Making provision for high quality experiences in the outdoor environment.* London, UK: Routledge.

Wilson, E. O. (1984). *Biophilia.* Cambridge, MA: Harvard University Press.

About the Author

Jennifer Quarrie is a dynamic innovation strategist and creativity expert with a visionary outlook and a knack for metacognition, facilitation, and listening. With a B.A. in Cognitive Science from the University of Virginia and an M.Sc. in Creative Studies from the International Center for Studies in Creativity at SUNY Buffalo State, she incorporates budding areas of mind and creativity research into all of her work. As a leader and speaker she inspires wellness, fosters transformation, and emboldens self-actualization.

Email: NurtureCreativeNature@gmail.com
Twitter: @JQVisionary

What If We View Our Education System as an Ecosystem?

Kathryn P. Haydon
International Center for Studies in Creativity
SUNY Buffalo State

Abstract

This paper introduces the Creative Learning Ecosystems model, which was developed using a biomimetic approach to education innovation. The model proposes a foundational structure from which the ideals of creative learning may be realized systemically on a micro or a macro scale. It is designed to illustrate to parents, schools, and organizations that the science of creativity can be used to delineate infrastructures that integrate content and rigorous creativity, and which result in engagement, learner motivation, continuous learning, and positive relationships among constituents. The author articulates the foundational creative learning framework, provides background on the systems model of creativity from which the model is derived, and translates this model into terminology and components related to education. Each component—person, process, press, product, and innovative change—is described as an element of the Creative Learning Ecosystem.

What If We View Our Education System as an Ecosystem?

Though never planted by human hands, the prairie is choked with blossoms, grasses gently pouring over, seeds setting, new shoots growing, runners criss-crossing the earth in a web of decay, growth, and new life. There is no hint of hail damage or drought wilt, no such thing as weeds. Every plant—231 species in this patch alone—has a role and cooperates with linked arms with the plants nearby. I see diversity of form—grasses splaying upward to different heights and widths, a sunflower's bold expanse, a legume's dark leaflets, fernlike in their repetition.

Benyus, 1997, p. 23

T he prairie, the natural state of the American plains, teems with life. It is an ecosystem diverse with plants whose individual strengths work in harmony to support the whole. Together, they prevail over harsh elements. Consider this image of a robust, dynamic, self-sustaining prairie: It is a healthy ecosystem of plants, insects, and other species sustaining each other and the land as they bend and wave in the wind.

Biomimicry draws on natural models and systems to help solve complex problems. What if we were to look through the biomimetic lens and study the prairie to inform best practices on nurturing and supporting learning? What if we were to view our education system as an ecosystem?

This paper explores the concept of creative learning as an ecosystem, supporting the call for creativity in the classroom articulated by Beghetto (2010): "[M]ost importantly, there is a need for creativity researchers to assist in the development, testing, and implementation of new pedagogical models that simultaneously support the development of creative potential and academic learning" (p. 459). It also introduces the Creative Learning Ecosystems model. Its theoretical background and related research support its potential to inform the design of sustainable learning infrastructures that integrate creativity and academic content.

Theoretical Foundation

What Is Creative Learning?

While the pedagogy of creative learning is not new, the term *creative learning* has recently gained traction in the United Kingdom, where several organizations contribute to an effort to bring such learning into classrooms throughout the country (Craft, Cremin, Burnard, & Chappell, 2007; Jeffrey & Craft, 2004). Worldwide, the term is still developing into a universally agreed-upon definition.

Broadly defined, creative learning is the integration of creativity, content, self-growth, and collaboration. Jeffrey's (2006) work comes closest to concisely articulating the pedagogy. He amplified his earlier research (Woods & Jeffrey, 2002) that placed creative learning within a humanitarian framework. In this paradigm, personal meaning and relevance to both learners and educators is essential, which follows Amabile's (1983) theory that creative tasks are driven by intrinsic motivation. Amabile's work was influenced by Torrance's (1979b) model, in which creative behavior arises at the intersection of motivation, skill, and abilities. Creative learning is rigorous because it exercises the highest stratum of thinking. Within the last decade, even Bloom's taxonomy (Bloom, Engelhart, Furst, Hill, & Krathwohl, 1956) has been revised to position creativity at the top level of thinking (Krathwohl, 2002). Torrance and Safter (1990) asserted that "the intuitive, creative thinking processes represent mankind's highest thinking ability" (p. 7).

Creative learning, then, can be characterized by four central assertions:

- Learning is meaningful to student interests and needs.

- Students are intrinsically motivated to learn.

- Creativity is integrated with academic content teaching and learning.

- The outcome is a change in thinking: new, meaningful ideas (sometimes expressed in the form of a product), skills, or personal growth.

When one is learning creatively, one is gaining meaningful self-knowledge. As Guilford (1977) stated, "Knowing the nature of your abilities, you will be able to turn them on when you need them and you will learn how to exercise them in order to strengthen them" (p. 12). This knowledge supports the development of solid individuals who are the pillars in a thriving creative learning ecosystem.

While there are scattered examples of schools that seem to function as creative learning ecosystems, these are the exception. Many roadblocks exist that schools perceive as barriers to adopting creative learning methodologies. For example, educators often do not know how to integrate an infrastructure of creative learning into content, assessment mandates, and curriculum standards. In addition, leaders at some schools feel they do incorporate creativity but do not have a way to measure or improve their practices. A rare handful of educators practice creative learning, but find it difficult to share their approaches, which are often developed intuitively. The Creative Learning Ecosystems model proposes a foundational structure from which the ideals of creative learning may be realized systemically on a micro or a macro scale.

Why Creative Learning?

A recent comprehensive literature review (Davies et al., 2013) of several hundred articles and studies concluded that creative learning significantly benefited students. Empirical studies included in the review demonstrated that creative learning led to learners' "improved academic achievement; increased confidence and resilience; enhanced motivation and engagement; development of social, emotional and thinking skills; and improved school attendance" (Davies et al., 2013, p. 88).

Creativity practitioners and researchers, in the past decade or so, have helped raise public awareness about creativity, intrinsic motivation, intelligence, engagement, and the need for a new educational paradigm (e.g., Amabile & Kramer, 2011; Florida, 2002; Robinson, 2009; Wagner, 2012). The essence of their message is that children begin with innate creativity, curiosity, and talents, and that traditional schooling methods tend to inhibit these characteristics and stifle the self in favor of conformity, an assertion that has been supported by decades of creativity research (Beghetto, 2010; Richards, 2010; Torrance, 1959; Wallach & Kogan, 1965). The message is beginning to resonate with more of the general public, due to widespread, accessible media platforms such as YouTube, Facebook, and the Internet in general. Even so, the literature from the field supporting the need for creativity as a central educational goal emerged in the 1950s and continues today in calling for a new educational paradigm that incorporates creative thinking (Beghetto, 2010; Craft et al., 2007; Cramond, Matthews-Morgan, Bandalos, & Zao, 2005; Guilford, 1950; Jeffrey, 2006; Kim, 2006; Krathwohl, 2002; Runco, Millar, Acar, & Cramond, 2010; Torrance, 1979a).

The majority of states in the United States have implemented the Common Core State Standards (CCSS). These standards claim to be "based on rigorous content and application of knowledge through higher-order thinking skills" (Common Core State Standards Initiative, n.d.-a). However, although creativity has been named the highest-level cognitive function (Krathwohl, 2002), a search of the term "creativity" on the CCSS website yields only one result, an off-hand reference buried in the high school math standards (Common Core State Standards Initiative, n.d.-b). Moreover, it has been demonstrated that methodologies such as the standardized assessments that have been developed to accompany the CCSS decrease the chance that creativity will thrive in the classroom (Beghetto, 2010). Studies (Beghetto, 2010; Sawyer, 2004) have shown that fact-based standardized tests beget fact-based, rote learning methodologies, narrower teaching practices and topics, and scripted curricula. Students in low-income areas are most likely to be negatively affected. A creative learning approach offers a strategy that supports higher-order thinking, academic learning, and self-knowledge across a spectrum of learners with widely different needs.

The Systems Model Influence

Over the last 50 years, creativity theories have advanced from a basic under-standing to a robust systems model that involves the intersection of Persons, Process, and Press (or environment), to effect a final outcome or Product (Puccio, Mance, & Murdock, 2011; Rhodes, 1961). In the organizational realm, each of these components must be carefully considered to drive new and useful products that, when implemented, create innovative change. The author asserts that to sustain creative learning, one must consider the interactions and connections among the people involved, the conditions of their press/environment (culture and climate as well as physical), and the processes used to facilitate learning. This holistic view is critical to informing the product or outcome: the depth of learning and growth experienced by learners, manifested in its meaningful application to their lives, which leads to change and fuels the iterative cycle of innovation and learning. The Creative Learning Ecosystems model is based on the systems model of creativity.

Creative Learning Ecosystems Model

Diversity allows a prairie to function successfully. The biological diversity of plants, grasses, insects, birds, and animals creates a complex web of interaction that makes the prairie resilient and robust. Species work together to contribute to the health and growth of the whole, and they do this by calling on their individual characteristics and adaptations. The prairie manifests—and often demands—individual growth and freedom of expression. The prairie leverages the adaptations that the species have developed over time, as well as the roles they play in the prairie organization. Only because it works as a system can it gracefully absorb harsh conditions such as flooding and strong winds. If the prairie forsook the primary contribution of each species in favor of fixing weaknesses first, the system would not function. When an outside force (such as humans) uproots individual species, the ecosystem deteriorates.

Similarly, creative learning ecosystems must center on learners by using built-in collaborative structures designed for maximum personal growth along a wide spectrum of intellectual diversity. This can be achieved only within a paradigm that acknowledges that each has a contribution to make and seeks to leverage these assets. Translating the components of the systems model of creativity to educational terminology, following is a description of what each means in an educational setting:

- Persons: instructor attitudes, outlooks, demeanor, approach; student attitudes and outlooks, often derived from instructor modeling; instructor view of students; parent attitudes and outlooks, often taken on cue from instructors

- Process: curriculum; course activities; structure of lesson plans; teaching methodologies

- Press: classroom climate, as determined by teacher norms, attitudes, atmosphere; classroom management practices; physical space

- Product: ideas and knowledge; products created by students that reflect new learning

- Innovation: application of learning to students' everyday lives; joy of learning; sense of progress

Understanding the relationship between education and the components of the systems model of creativity involves how they work together as an interconnected network. Figure 1 depicts the Creative Learning Ecosystems Model. Expanding on the model, Table 1 details each component of the ecosystem, describes its function, and relates it to the systems model of creativity. An elaboration of each component follows, and an exploration of how they all fit within the creative learning ecosystem.

Learners and Leaders, Partners, and Individuals

Like the prairie, the strength of a learning ecosystem begins with finding the positive contributions that each individual has the potential to make. There are three significant categories of individuals involved: educators (teachers and administrators), students, and parents. In a creative learning ecosystem, it is essential to value, acknowledge, and engage their respective strengths to sustain the cycle of continuous learning and growth.

The success of learning in a classroom or a school begins with transformational leadership as modeled by teachers and administrators. A key component of this

Creative Learning Ecosystem

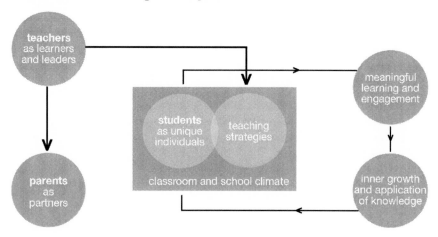

Figure 1. A diagram of the Creative Learning Ecosystems model. Adapted from Puccio, G. J., Mance, M., & Murdock, M. C. (2011). *Creative leadership: Skills that drive change* (2nd ed.). Thousand Oaks, CA: Sage.

type of leadership is valuing the creative characteristics and growth of oneself and others:

> The transformational leader recognizes the inherent value and benefit in promoting individual creativity.... Through their behavior, they create a work climate that supports others' creativity, encouraging followers to pursue their own solutions to problems, to explore complex challenges by reframing problems, and to question decisions and practices. (Puccio et al., 2011, pp. 14-15)

The theory of transformational leadership values creativity as a core leadership quality as well as an outcome. Leaders are most effective when they express characteristics of creativity such as awareness, playfulness, improvisation, joy, curiosity, courage, inspiration, intuition, freedom, humor, and perceptivity (Puccio et al., 2011). Relationships in this paradigm must be built on a platform of mutual respect (Davies et al., 2013).

Educators accept the role that each individual plays in the ecosystem and what they contribute; this includes the need to accept highly creative students who often are misunderstood, penalized for their divergent thinking, or are not well-liked by teachers in traditional classrooms (Kim, 2009; Richards, 2010;

Systems Model of Creativity	Creative Learning Ecosystems Model	
	Label	Description
Persons	Teachers as learners and leaders	Instructor attitudes, outlooks, demeanor, approach
	Parents as partners	Parent attitudes and outlooks, often taken on cue from instructors
	Students as unique individuals	Attitudes and outlooks, often derived from instructor modeling; instructor view of students
Process	Teaching strategies	Curriculum; course activities; structure of lesson plans; teaching methodologies
Press/ Environment	Classroom and school climate and culture	Classroom climate, as determined by teacher norms, attitudes, atmosphere; classroom management practices; physical space
Product	Meaningful learning and engagement	Ideas and knowledge gained that are new and meaningful to students; products created by students that reflect new learning
Innovation	Inner growth and application of knowledge	Application of ideas to students' everyday lives; joy of learning; sense of progress

Table 1. Table depicting each component of the Creative Learning Ecosystems model, its function, and its relationship to the systems model of creativity.

Wallach & Kogan, 1965). These students are akin to species such as trees that grow on the edges of the prairie.

Those who study prairies are often fascinated with the edges, because they are unpredictable and interesting. Prairie expert Mike Fox explained its appeal: "The edges of things are the most visually challenging or interesting, like between concrete and grass. The edge can be a problem or an opportunity because there is no longer a monolithic set of material" (J. M. Fox, personal communication, August 15, 2013). As such, outlier students should be valued for their strengths. For all students, specific feedback can make a significant difference in their lives and growth. Beghetto (2010) observed, "One of the most direct and potentially influential ways that teachers can support the development of students' creative self-efficacy beliefs is to provide informative feedback on their creative potential and ability" (p. 458). When teachers respond positively to the creative activity of their students, creativity is perpetuated (Davies et al., 2013).

Parents are integral to the creative learning ecosystem. Though some researchers cite the lack of consistent empirical results (Fan & Chen, 2001), personal experience strongly affirms that student success is positively influenced by healthy school-home communication. Within the realm of creative learning, parental support is important. Smutny, Haydon, Bolaños, and Danley (2012) asserted that parents "need to know what the classroom teacher is doing in order to play a supportive role in the home" (p. 94). To truly support the creative growth of students, it is critical that educators view parents as partners in the process, and this responsibility falls squarely on the shoulders of educational leadership (including teachers) to set a collaborative tone. Educators need parent insights, and parents need educator insights in order to accurately meet the needs of the students. Often, parents see a very different child at home than is witnessed at school. Dawson (1997) affirmed, "The research does suggest that teachers should listen seriously to parents who claim that their child performs creatively in settings other than school" (p. 151). This information can be leveraged to help engage a child and support his or her learning. When schools and teachers minimize the role of parents, or shut them out for fear of being criticized or controlled, they spawn mistrust and suspicion. The parent is less likely to support the work of the teacher when he or she does not know what is going on in the classroom. The entire ecosystem, including student learning, suffers as a consequence.

Teaching Strategies and Curriculum

Curriculum strategies in a creative learning ecosystem look vastly different from the convergent teaching strategies that seek single right answers and dominate classrooms worldwide (Beghetto, 2010). Creative learning best practices include: authentic projects and problem solving that students perceive as valuable; a balance between structure and freedom of choice; flexibility in time use, including allowing individuals to work at their own pace; clear expectations; opportunities to explore, imagine, discover, invent, and draw original conclusions; novelty; a mix of work and play; field trips outside of the classroom, including the use of outdoor space; and professional visitors and mentors to the classroom (Davies et al., 2013; Torrance & Goff, 1990).

A promising framework to easily integrate creativity and content is the Torrance Incubation Model of Teaching and Learning (Torrance, 1979a), which has seen a recent resurgence in research and application (Cramond, 2013; Keller-Mathers, 2009, in press; Keller-Mathers & Murdock, 2002). Additionally, best practices from the field of gifted education can be applied within the context of creativity and content integration. More than two decades ago, Torrance and Safter (1990) wrote, "Gifted education has nurtured the creativity movement until it is now shared by all areas of education" (p. 3). In the ensuing 25 years, this sharing has become more and more of a reality.

Creative learning necessitates a variety of assessment methods, including creative products. Besemer (1984, 2006) and Besemer and O'Quin (1987) provided foundational work that demonstrated how to assess creative products; such assessments can be built into a rubric that clearly communicates the expectation that students contribute creativity and original thought (Keller-Mathers, 2007, in press). This assessment structure ensures that creativity is not included in name only, but is maintained as a central value held by the teacher leader.

The Classroom and School Environment

Culture, climate, and physical space are three environmental dimensions. Culture and climate are derived from leadership practices and teaching processes. In the educational realm, culture can be roughly defined as school and classroom management practices. Climate can be roughly characterized as the spirit in which teachers respond to students and their ideas, which in turn sets the tone for how students respond to each other. Ekvall (1996) identified measurable dimensions of the creative environment, including freedom, idea time, idea support, challenge, lack of conflict, playfulness/humor, trust/openness, risk-taking, debate, and liveliness. These dimensions clearly overlap with best practices described elsewhere in this paper.

A comprehensive review of the literature related to creative learning environments (Davies et al., 2013) further delineated their essential aspects. The physical environment should be a flexible space that can be changed according to specific needs that arise to best support student creativity. Additional characteristics of an effective creative learning space include openness, small spaces embedded in the overall space, display of student work in progress, use of outdoor space, and access to a wide range of materials and resources, including technology.

Meaningful Learning and Engagement

Some models of creativity and creative learning have defined the "product" aspect to be a tangible piece of work produced by the student (Smith & Smith, 2010). However, this author and others (e.g., Puccio, Mance, & Murdock, 2011) have adopted an expansive view which asserts that the outcome of creative learning may be an actual product, or it may be an idea, which includes new, meaningful learning or insight to oneself in the realm of mini-c creativity (Craft et al., 2007; Kaufman & Beghetto, 2009). Torrance designed his incubation model on just this premise. Each phase of each lesson elicits student curiosity and a desire to dig deeper. He wrote, "For creative thinking to occur and to continue to occur, there must be ample opportunity for one thing to lead to another, and to do something with the information encountered" (Torrance, 1979a, p. 31). There is always a way to give students the opportunity to continue to think about what they have learned and to apply it further. In order for this continued incubation and application to occur, meaning must have been created for the student in the process.

Inner Growth and Application of Knowledge

The prairie is the site of an iterative process that cycles precipitation through the system to create more precipitation, which thereby regulates temperatures and moisture (Savage, 2011). The joy of learning, the satisfaction in attaining greater self-knowledge through learning application, the tangible progress reflected in creative products, and a feeling of collaboration, drive a similar iterative cycle within a creative learning ecosystem. This feeds each dimension of the system so that it can be sustained and reinvigorated over time.

Conclusion

To our knowledge there has not been articulated a systematic model such as the one proposed here, which serves as a framework to develop creative learning infrastructures, and which can be applied on both a micro level (to homes, individual classrooms, and schools) and a macro level (in large districts, and at the level of public policy).

Such a systems approach appears essential to the long-term sustainability of rigorous creativity in education. For example, in an educational system dominated by test taking and homogenization, it is virtually impossible for an individual teacher to sustain a creative learning platform over the long haul. This would be akin to planting a single prairie grass seed in the midst of a manicured garden of annuals. The seed would not have the ecosystem of support needed to grow. It is more plausible for a single school to do so, but still there exist enormous societal pressures to regress toward the mean. Certainly, there are programs and initiatives nationwide that have elements in common with the Creative Learning Ecosystems model; however, as a comprehensive model, it is in its earliest stages. It should be populated with best practices and further researched to create a detailed map that can guide educators to create self-sustaining creative learning ecosystems that can better weather changes in politics, policy, and public opinion.

References

Amabile, T. M. (1983). The social psychology of creativity: A componential conceptualization. *Journal of Personality and Social Psychology, 45*(2), 357-376.

Amabile, T., & Kramer, S. (2011). *The progress principle.* Boston, MA: Harvard Business Review Press.

Beghetto, R. A. (2010). Creativity in the classroom. In J. C. Kaufman & R. J. Sternberg (Eds.), *The Cambridge handbook of creativity* (pp. 447-463). New York, NY: Cambridge University Press.

Benyus, J. (1997). *Biomimicry.* New York, NY: William Morrow.

Besemer, S. (1984). How do you know it's creative? *Gifted Child Today, 32*, 30-35.

Besemer, S. (2006). *Creating products in the age of design.* Stillwater, OK: New Forums.

Besemer, S., & O'Quin, K. (1987). Creative product analysis. In S. G. Isaksen (Ed.), *Frontiers of creativity research: Beyond the basics* (pp. 341-357). Buffalo, NY: Bearly Limited.

Bloom, B. S., Engelhart, M. D., Furst, E. J., Hill, W. H., & Krathwohl, D. R. (Eds.) (1956). *Taxonomy of educational objectives: The classification of educational goals. Handbook 1: Cognitive domain.* New York, NY: David McKay.

Common Core State Standards Initiative (n.d.-a). *About the Common Core State Standards.* Retrieved from http://www.corestandards.org/about-the-standards

Common Core State Standards Initiative (n.d.-b). *High School: Modeling.* Retrieved from http://www.corestandards.org/Math/Content/HSM

Craft, A., Cremin, T., Burnard, P., & Chappell, K. (2007). Teacher stance in creative learning: A study of progression. *Thinking Skills and Creativity, 2*(2), 136-147.

Cramond, B. (2013). The life and contributions of E. Paul Torrance. In E. Romey (Ed.), *Finding John Galt: People, politics, and practice in gifted education* (pp. 25-31). Charlotte, NC: Information Age Publishing.

Cramond, B., Matthews-Morgan, J., Bandalos, D., & Zuo, L. (2005). A report on the 40-year follow-up of the Torrance Tests of Creative Thinking: Alive and well in the new millennium. *Gifted Child Quarterly, 49*(4), 283-291.

Davies, D., Jindal-Snape, D., Collier, C., Digby, R., Hay, P., & Howe, A. (2013). Creative learning environments in education—A systematic literature review. *Thinking Skills and Creativity, 8,* 80-91.

Dawson, V. L. (1997). In search of the wild Bohemian: Challenges in the identification of the creatively gifted. *Roeper Review, 19,* 148-152.

Ekvall, G. (1996). Organizational climate for creativity and innovation. *European Journal of Work and Organizational Psychology, 5,* 105-123.

Fan, X., & Chen, M. (2001). Parental involvement and students' academic achievement: A meta-analysis. *Educational Psychology Review, 13*(1), 1-22.

Florida, R. (2012). *The rise of the creative class, revisited.* New York, NY: Basic Books.

Guilford, J. P. (1950). Creativity. *American Psychologist, 5,* 444-454.

Guilford, J. P. (1977). *Way beyond the IQ: Guide to improving intelligence and creativity.* Buffalo, NY: Creative Education Foundation.

Jeffrey, B. (2006). Creative teaching and learning: Towards a common discourse and practice. *Cambridge Journal of Education, 36*(3), 399-414.

Jeffrey, B., & Craft, A. (2004). Teaching creatively and teaching for creativity: Distinctions and relationships. *Educational Studies, 30*(1), 77-87.

Kaufman, J. C., & Beghetto, R. A. (2009). Beyond big and little: The Four C Model of creativity. *Review of General Psychology, 13*(1), 1-12.

Keller-Mathers, S. (2007, February). *Blending expertise and imagination: The essential creativity ingredient in gifted education.* Paper presented at the Colorado Department of Education State Director's Conference, Denver, CO.

Keller-Mathers, S. (2009). Creative teaching. In B. Kerr (Ed.), *Encyclopedia of giftedness, creativity, and talent* (pp. 197-200). Thousand Oaks, CA: Sage.

Keller-Mathers, S. (In press). *The curious classroom: Weaving creativity into content with TIM.* Buffalo, NY: ICSC Press.

Keller-Mathers, S., & Murdock, M. C. (2002). Teaching the content of creativity using the Torrance Incubation Model: Eyes wide open to the possibilities of learning. *National Association of Gifted Children's Celebrate Creativity, 12*(2), 7-9.

Kim, K. H. (2006). Can we trust creativity tests? A review of the Torrance Tests of Creative Thinking (TTCT). *Creativity Research Journal, 18*(1), 3-14.

Kim, K. H. (2009). The two pioneers of research on creative giftedness: Calvin W. Taylor and E. Paul Torrance. In L. Shavinina (Ed.), *International handbook on giftedness* (pp. 571-583). Dordrecht, Netherlands: Springer.

Krathwohl, D. (2002). A revision of Bloom's Taxonomy: An overview. *Theory into Practice, 41*(4), 212-218.

Puccio, G. J., Mance, M., & Murdock, M. C. (2011). *Creative leadership: Skills that drive change* (2nd ed.). Thousand Oaks, CA: Sage.

Rhodes, M. (1961). An analysis of creativity. *The Phi Delta Kappan, 42*(7), 305-310.

Richards, R. (2010). Everyday creativity: Process and way of life—four key issues. In J. C. Kaufman & R. J. Sternberg (Eds.), *The Cambridge handbook of creativity* (pp. 189-215). New York, NY: Cambridge University Press.

Robinson, K. (2009). *The element: How finding your passion changes everything.* New York, NY: Viking.

Runco, M. A., Millar, G., Acar, S., & Cramond, B. (2010). Torrance Tests of Creative Thinking as predictors of personal and public achievement: A fifty-year follow-up. *Creativity Research Journal, 22*(4), 361-368.

Savage, C. (2011). *Prairie: A natural history* (2nd ed.). Vancouver, BC: Greystone Books.

Sawyer, R. K. (2004). Creative teaching: Collaborative discussion as disciplined improvisation. *Educational Researcher, 33*, 12-20.

Smith, J. K., & Smith, L. F. (2010). Educational creativity. In J. C. Kaufman & R. J. Sternberg (Eds.), *The Cambridge handbook of creativity* (pp. 250-264). New York, NY: Cambridge University Press.

Smutny, J. F., Haydon, K. P., Bolaños, O., & Danley, G. E. (2012). *Discovering and developing talents in Spanish-speaking students.* Thousand Oaks, CA: Corwin.

Torrance, E. P. (1959). Current research on the nature of creative talent. *Journal of Counseling Psychology, 6*(4), 309-316.

Torrance, E. P. (1979a). An instructional model for enhancing incubation. *Journal of Creative Behavior, 13*(1), 23-35.

Torrance, E. P. (1979b). *The search for satori and creativity.* Buffalo, NY: Creative Education Foundation.

Torrance, E. P., & Goff, K. (1990). Fostering academic creativity in gifted students. *ERIC Digest #E484.* Retrieved from http://eric.ed.gov/?id=ED321489

Torrance, E. P., & Safter, H. T. (1990). *The incubation model of teaching.* Buffalo, NY: Bearly Limited.

Wagner, T. (2012). *Creating innovators: The making of young people who will change the world.* New York, NY: Scribner.

Wallach, M. A., & Kogan, N. (1965). A new look at the creativity-intelligence distinction. *Journal of Personality, 33*(3), 348-369.

Woods, P., & Jeffrey, B. (2002). The reconstruction of primary teachers' identities. *British Journal of Sociology in Education, 23*(1), 89-106.

About the Author

Kathryn P. Haydon, founder of Sparkitivity, is an innovative educator and consultant who speaks and writes widely on education and creativity, including co-authoring *Creativity for Everybody* (Sparkitivity, 2015) and *Discovering and Developing Talents in Spanish-Speaking Students* (Corwin, 2012). She holds an M.S. in Creativity from the International Center for Studies in Creativity at SUNY Buffalo State, a B.A. from Northwestern University, and is a published poet.

Website: http://sparkitivity.com
Facebook: https://www.facebook.com/sparkitivity
Creativity Post: http://www.creativitypost.com/authors/list/152/khaydon

Can We Meaningfully Compare Creativity Across Cultures?

Gaia Grant
International Center for Studies in Creativity
SUNY Buffalo State

Abstract

Investigating the relationship between creativity and culture can provide valuable insights into creative thinking and innovation. An examination of different cultural experiences of creativity reveals that although some useful distinctions can be made between cultures, it becomes clear that many common contemporary assumptions about creativity may have been derived from distinctly Western perspectives, which are not necessarily universally shared. A deeper exploration of the development of creativity and innovation throughout history reveals that although some cultures avail themselves of technological innovation, different cultures are creative in different ways. Creative thinking is a critical survival skill, and innovation can and should provide the means of improving the lives of people around the world. The challenge for the future will be to ensure that cultures learn from each other and share the diversity of creative thinking and innovation for the benefit of all.

Can We Meaningfully Compare Creativity Across Cultures?

A billboard on display at airports around the world shows two photos of people with elaborate tattoos. Labeled "Trendy" and "Traditional," the photos imply that a specific form of creative expression may be seen one way in one culture, and quite differently in another. As a part of an advertising campaign from the bank HSBC, the billboard identifies cultural differences via simple visual images and upends potentially biased perceptions.

The HSBC campaign demonstrates the profound relationship between creativity and culture. The two are intricately intertwined, and it is impossible to truly understand one without attempting to understand the other. As John Eger (2013), director of the Creative Economy Initiative at San Diego State University, has summarized from a number of quotes, culture is essential to understanding creativity and creativity is essential to understanding culture. Eger noted that Irina Bokova, Director General of UNESCO, stated in 2013 that "Culture...is a wellspring of innovation and creativity," while the European Commission's Directorate for Education and Culture reversed the relationship, saying: "Culture is the general expression of humanity, the expression of its creativity." Eger also quotes John Lobell, professor of architecture at Pratt Institute, as saying that "Visionary creativity...is embedded in its culture, and at the same time remakes its culture."

In the world's 196 countries live some 2,000 ethnic-natural groups, and about 5,000 distinct peoples (International Work Group on Indigenous Affairs, 2005). This enriching diversity naturally extends to creativity. All cultures express and apply creativity—as well as in the very ways they think about creativity—differently. Rather than comparing and contrasting, a common approach in the past, I aim to collect and synthesize ideas into a tapestry of concepts that can underpin future understanding and development, and perhaps enhance our ability to innovate and advance as a global community.

Defining and Developing Creativity

The etymology of the word "creativity" derives from the Indo-European root *ker/kere*, which means "to grow," into the Latin word *creatio* or *creare* (to make or grow). In its modern context, the word was first used in 1875 by Adolfus William Ward in his *History of Dramatic English Literature* to describe Shakespeare's poetry (Ward, 1901). Yet it was only after WWII that the word was common enough in English to be included in the English dictionary (Weiner, 2000).

Kaufman and Sternberg (2006) have revealed that the first "creativity training" programs were introduced by the General Electric Corporation in the mid-1930s; and the concept of "creative problem solving" first emerged in the release of Alex Osborn's (1948) book *Your Creative Power*. Around the same time, they say, creativity was determined to be an important aspect of a healthy personality. Since then, creativity has been the subject of empirical study in multiple fields.

Despite the recognition of the concept in the West, cultures elsewhere exist that do not have an equivalent word for creativity. In their survey of 28 African languages, Mpofu, Myambo, Mogaji, Mashego, and Khaleefa (2006) found that only one, Arabic, had a word which directly translated to "creativity."

The concept of creativity may have become connected to certain political and value systems linked to specific countries and cultures. As Sternberg and Lubart (1999) maintained, most Western scholars agree that a creative product must be novel as well as useful. Many also say it must be of value (Murray, 1959), or that it should benefit someone or something (Mason, 1960). Montaigne noted in 1580 that "strangeness and novelty...generally give things value" (Frame, 1943). According to Weiner (2000), this accepted definition appears to link creativity to capitalism, a political system generally associated with the West. Schumpeter (1975) originally related creativity to capitalism through the concept of creative destruction.

Although similar designations of creativity as novel and original thinking can be found in both Eastern and Western cultures (Lim & Plucker, 2001), subtle differences arise between what is meant by "novel." Sternberg, Kaufman, and Pretz (2002) identified "novel" as any of the following: (1) reiterating a known idea in a new way, (2) moving a field forward along its current trajectory, (3) moving a field forward in a new direction, or (4) leading to an iteration of diverse trends in a field. While the second and third aspects might fit better with the Western view of novelty, the first and fourth appear to fit more closely with the Eastern view. These differences underscore why it is difficult to make direct comparisons between cultures.

"Cultural Gestalt" and Generalizations

Identifying differences between cultures can lead to generalizations—helpful on one hand in assisting with cross-cultural appreciation, but possibly harmful on the other.

Hofstede (1983) established a set of principles by which it is possible to define and compare cultures. Hofstede's dimensions emerged from a landmark study of IBM across more than 70 countries. The six cultural dimensions represent preferences for one state of affairs over another, and which distinguishes countries (rather than individuals) from each other. The dimensions are: power distance, uncertainty avoidance (versus acceptance), individualism versus collectivism, masculinity versus femininity, long-term versus short-term orientation, and indulgence versus restraint. In a study of 62 societies, House, Hanges, Javidan, Dorfman, and Gupta (2004), investigated some of these dimensions and more: assertiveness, future orientation, gender egalitarianism, human orientation, institutional collectivism, performance orientation, power distance, and uncertainty avoidance. While these sorts of dimensions have become a benchmark for cross-cultural comparisons, generalizations are misleading for two reasons. First, all cultures are unique. Second, all cultures are all rapidly transitioning, so it is more and more difficult to easily categorize them.

Lubart (2010) warned about the danger of generalizing to the point of "cultural gestalt," saying that because cultures are so complex they cannot be easily be reduced to generalizations. Table 1 details some common comparisons between Eastern and Western cultures, as identified by a number of researchers examining psychological and social aspects of creativity.

In terms of the key characteristics of creative people, most cultures agree on the necessity of specific cognitive and personality skills, and motivational attributes such as imagination, self-confidence, and enthusiasm (Kaufman & Sternberg, 2006; Rudowicz, 2003). Moreover, most cultures commonly view creativity as an adaptive value as well as a social utility (Lubart, 2010).

As previously mentioned, these comparisons are helpful insofar as they help to foster cultural understanding and appreciation. They can, however, become harmful when a weighted value is placed on the differences.

Table 1: Cultural comparisons of various creativity concepts

Level	East	West
Individual / psychological	Emptying our minds and lives (Weiner, 2000)	Filling our minds and lives with knowledge and possessions (Bereiter, 2005)
	Achieving success in creativity through performing rituals (Pye, 2000)	Success through hard work (Pye, 2000)
	Intrinsic values (Grondona, 2000)	Instrumental values (Grondona, 2000)
	Not humor-related (Rudowicz, 2003)	Humor-related (Rudowicz, 2003)
	Creativity related to wisdom (Mpofu et al., 2006)	Creativity separate from wisdom (Mpofu et al., 2006)
	Emotional control (Runco, 2004)	Emotional expression (Runco, 2004)
	Focus on the process; "cyclic, nonlinear and enlightening" (e.g., Hinduism and classical Chinese) creativity can be expressing a well-known topic in a new way (Westwood & Low, 2003)	Focus on product (Westwood & Low, 2003; Niu & Sternberg, 2002/2003); fits with the concept of linear movement toward a new point (von Franz, 1995)
	Success through rituals to increase good luck; the authenticity of the discovery process (Pye, 2000)	Success through hard work, and through the output (Pye, 2000)
	Creativity is an inner state of fulfillment; meditation is a way of seeing the true nature (Chu, 1970)	Creativity is an action (Joas & Kilpinen, 2006)
	Focus on cognitive skills, e.g., in Korea (Lubart, 2010)	Focus on personality and motivational factors (Lubart, 2010)
Social	Community; define the self within the social context (Lubart & Georgsdottir, 2004)	Individuality; define the self as autonomous (Lubart & Georgsdottir, 2004)
	Creativity can be expressed by groups or even whole communities, e.g., Kung San (Shostak, 1993), African communities (Mpofu et al., 2006)	Creativity is expressed by individuals (Puccio & Grivas, 2009)
	Emphasis on conformity (Runco, 2004)	Emphasis on autonomy and freedom (Runco, 2004)
	Creativity seen as deviant quality (Chan & Chan, 1999; Lim & Plucker, 2001; Lubart, 2010; Raina, 1975; Raina & Raina, 1971)	Creativity seen as admirable quality (Runco & Johnson, 2002)
	Innovation through incremental change (Lubart & Georgsdottir, 2004; Urabe, Child & Kagono, 1988)	Innovation through radical transformation (Lubart & Georgsdottir, 2004; Urabe, Child, & Kagono, 1988)
	Creativity can be seen in domains of science and politics (Niu & Kaufman, 2005)	Creativity can be seen in the domain of art (Puccio, Mance, Switalski, & Reali, 2012)

Breaking Through Biases

A number of popularly held Western assumptions about creativity persist. One is that creativity is related to self-actualization. Rogers (1961) said:

> The mainspring of creativity appears to be the same tendency which we discover so deeply as the curative force in psychotherapy—one's tendency to actualize oneself, to become one's potentials...the urge to expand, extend, develop, mature—the tendency to express and activate all of the capabilities of the organism. (p. 65)

Maslow (1971) elaborated: "My feeling is that the concept of creativeness and the concept of the healthy, self-actualizing, fully human person seem to be coming closer together, and may perhaps turn out to be the same thing"(p. 57).

Csikszentmihalyi's (1990) concept of flow as a heightened state of creativity underscored this link. According to Maslow's "hierarchy of needs" theory (1968), people must deal with the basic physiological and safety needs before being able to progress to the higher-order need of self-actualization. This means that, in many societies, people are not in a position to contemplate the idea of self-actualization, let alone experience it.

And then, from another angle, there are still today countries such as China where independence, creative thinking, and self-expression—to say nothing of self-actualization—are censored or lead to imprisonment, and nearly anything that contradicts government policy is forbidden (Weiner, 2000). Creativity and tradition may conflict so that while a culture remains traditional, it may be difficult for it to become more creative.

One of the more fascinating concepts related to creativity is the idea of Jugaad innovation (Radjou, Prabhu, Ahaju, & Roberts, 2012). First identified in Asia, and more recently applied in business contexts, Jugaad outlines how a number of cultures have had to learn to be creative to survive. This concept of ad-hoc innovation and flexibility borne from necessity, which might be expected to apply to small-scale innovations, has now reached into space (Schomer, 2014). Innovation, in this viewpoint, is not simply about self-actualization, individual development, or product or technical development; rather, it is a form of creative thinking that ensures individuals and communities can deal with challenges.

Driving Ahead: Creativity, Innovation and Progress

Differences in views on creativity over the years have no doubt affected innovation—which has, in turn, impacted development. It is therefore important to understand how these differences may have originated and what effect they might have in the future.

Diamond (2012) holds that the developmental differences between societies through the ages is due to environmental variances. The ancient peoples living near the Fertile Crescent had the animals and plants that were best suited to domestication, and therefore they were able to grow from bands to states, and to expand throughout the world more easily. They also advanced faster technologically due to the access to more resources.

The technological gap between advanced and lagging countries has tended to widen rather than narrow over time. As Sachs (2000) stated, "Technological innovation operates like a chain reaction in which current innovations provide the fuel for future breakthroughs" (p. 30). Sachs claimed these positive feedback mechanisms explained differences in economic growth between countries.

The Organisation for Economic Cooperation and Development (OECD; 1994) created a regionalized directory of patents in order to assess the development between countries. This has provided insight into the comparative development of creativity and innovation (Maurat, Dernis, Webb, Spiezia, & Guellec, 2008). The OECD report found that the most important differentiating factors seem to be rural versus urban factors. An analysis of this data by Rothwell (2012) identified the overwhelming dominance of cities and metropolitan areas in the generation of global innovations. He found that metropolitan areas supported 93 percent of the world's patent applications, with only 23 percent of the world's population.

Lehrer (2010) described how all of the 10 most highly innovative metro areas (in order, Tokyo, San Jose, New York, Boston, Kanagawa (Japan), Shenzhen (China), Osaka, San Diego, Los Angeles, and Seoul) which have large or very large populations when considering their surrounding metro areas. That allows their workers and researchers to become highly specialized in their jobs, which in turn fosters innovation. Bettencourt, Lobo, Helbing, Kuhnert, and West (2007) have reinforced that innovation often thrives in large cities with more connections and opportunities.

Toward a Global Village

The global cultural climate is changing rapidly as people become more closely connected through more advanced technology and communications. I believe as a number of countries and cultures emerge from their traditional past and move rapidly into a "modern" future, cultures will change dramatically, and the differences in experiences and perspectives on creativity will decrease rapidly. I further believe these changes will mostly be influenced by the values of the West.

As the world moves toward becoming a global village (McLuhan & Fiore, 1968), varied ideas and principles are beginning to blend. Lau, Hui, and Ng (2004) said that the traditionally Western (and specifically American) values of individuality and imagination have already been found to be prized over community and communalism by young people in a number of Asian countries today, particularly in Hong Kong, mainland China, and Singapore.

Habermas (1991) posited the theory that the world would become an international society with individuals communicating with each other across countries and cultures. The Internet embodies this theory. Weiner (2000) described an "electronic superhighway" that encircles the world, effecting a change in people's universal experience of creativity:

> Millions of people around the world now share a virtually infinite diversity and quantity of ideas. The Internet has reinforced the contemporary idea of creativity coming from anyone, anywhere, at any time; it has sped up our lives and brought us further along toward the merger of information, entertainment, technology, and art, a new way of communicating, and to some extent, a new way of being. (p. 107)

I feel that a cross-pollination of ideas due to closer contact, more international education opportunities, and global media exposure have led to greater homogenization. Because of this, I believe the shift in values towards the Western ideal has become a worldwide phenomenon.

Many countries have been changed by this phenomenon. For example, Singapore is ranked as one of the world's most innovative countries (Elnhorn, 2009; Bloomberg, 2014). It came into being through the deliberate amalgamation of three dominant traditional cultures—Chinese, Indian, and Malaysian—and its future-focused leadership has steered the country toward significant Western-style technological and social advances. The country continues to attempt to balance repressive political control with creative freedom (The Guardian, 2010).

China is also a culture in transition, with the challenge of an even more traditional and closed power base. Deng Xiaoping, leader of China from 1978 to 1992, recognized the need to modernize the economy through an open-door policy known as *kai fang zhengee*. This allowed the establishment of small scale-capitalism through setting up domestic enterprise zones (Ho & Huenemann, 1984). As China has attempted to cultivate more creativity, it has also attempted to democratize the governmental process in order to make it possible.

I feel it will be interesting to see how these and other countries fare as they continue to change, and whether they will inevitably move toward the Western ideal of creativity or forge their own original path.

Conclusion

My initial question might be taken to assume that there could be greater and lesser cultures—as well as winners and losers—when it comes to creativity and innovation. Yet I believe it should be possible to accept the vast variations in creativity and innovation, allowing all cultures to embrace them all, at least to some extent.

Lau, Hui, and Ng (2004) claimed that the West typically simplifies Eastern ideologies such as Confucianism and collectivism to explain the differences in creativity. They maintained that these philosophies are then tied to a number of preconceived notions, such as conformity, group-orientation, face-saving, etc., which are all identified as being detrimental to the development of creativity. On the other hand, they say, no similar attempt is made in the West to simplify the ideologies of the United States.

Hofstede, Hofstede, and Minkov (2010) identified that when people speak about alien cultures, they often refer to them in moral terms, as better or worse. Yet, as they maintained, "There are no scientific standards for considering the ways of thinking, feeling and acting of one group as intrinsically superior or inferior to those of another" (Hofstede et al., 2010, p. 25). Furthermore, Ng & Smith (2004) have held that although cultures differ, they cannot and should not be directly compared.

Now that many individuals and cultures are respecting the values that different cultures bring, I feel that this respect may lead to the need to find equilibrium in the midst of ambiguity. Weiner (2000) claimed that creativity is, in fact, *the* contemporary value for the global village, naming it a "currency of exchange between conservatives and liberals, Americans and Asians, businesspeople and artists" (p. 111).

References

Bereiter, C. (2005). *Education and mind in the knowledge age.* London, GB: Routledge.

Bettencourt, L. M. A., Lobo, J., Helbing, D., Kuhnert, C., & West, G. B. (2007). Growth, innovation, scaling, and the pace of life in cities. *Proceedings of the National Academy of Science, 104*(17), 7301-7306. doi:10.1073/pnas.0610172104

Bloomberg (2014). *Most innovative in the world 2014: Countries* [Data file]. Retrieved from http://images.businessweek.com/bloomberg/pdfs/most_innovative_countries_2014_011714.pdf

Chan, D. W., & Chan, L. K. (1999). Implicit theories of creativity: Teachers' perception of student characteristics in Hong Kong. *Creativity Research Journal, 12(3)*, 185-195.

Chu, Y. K. (1970). Oriental views on creativity. *Psi factors in creativity,* 35-50.

Csikszentmihalyi, M. (1990). *Flow: The psychology of optimal experience.* New York, NY: Harper and Row.

De Montaigne, M. (1958). *The complete essays of Montaigne.* Stanford, CA: Stanford University Press.

Diamond, J. (2012). *The world until yesterday: What can we learn from traditional societies?* London, UK: Viking.

Eger, J. M. (2013, November 9). *Culture may be the key to creativity.* Retrieved from http://www.huffingtonpost.com/john-m-eger/culture-may-be-the-key-to_b_4305732.html

Elnhorn, B. (2009, March 16). *Innovation: Singapore is no. 1, well ahead of the US.* Retrieved from http://www.businessweek.com/globalbiz/content/mar2009/gb20090316_004837.htm

Fabun, D. (1968). *You and creativity.* New York, NY: Macmillan.

Frame, D. M. (1943). *The complete works of Montaigne.* Stanford, CA: Leland Stanford Junior University.

Grondona, M. (2000). A cultural typology of economic development. In L. E. Harrison & S. P. Huntington (Eds.) *Culture matters: How values shape human progress.* New York, NY: Basic Books.

Habermas, J. (1991). *Moral consciousness and communicative action.* Cambridge, MA: MIT Press.

Ho, S. P. S., & Huenemann, R. (1984). *China's open door policy: The quest for foreign technology and capital.* Vancouver, BC: University of British Columbia Press.

Hofstede, G. (1983). Culture's consequences: International differences in work-related values. *Administrative Science Quarterly, 28(4),* 625-629.

Hofstede, G., Hofstede, G. J., & Minkov, M. (2010). *Cultures and organizations: Software of the mind.* New York, NY: McGraw-Hill.

House, R. J., Hanges, P. J., Javidan, M., Dorfman, P. W., & Gupta, V. (2004). *Culture, leadership and organizations: The GLOBE study of 62 societies.* Thousand Oaks, CA: Sage.

International Work Group on Indigenous Affairs (2005). *Indigenous issues.* Retrieved from http://www.iwgia.org/

Joas, H. & Kilpinen, E. (2006). Creativity and society. In J. R. Shook & J. Margolis (Eds.), *A companion to pragmatism* (pp. 323-335). Malden, MA: Wiley-Blackwell.

Kaufman, J. C., & Sternberg R. J. (Eds.) (2006). *The international handbook of creativity.* New York, NY: Cambridge University Press.

Lau, S., Hui, A. N. N., & Ng, G. Y. C. (2004). *Creativity: When East meets West.* Danvers, MA: World Scientific Publishing.

Lehrer, J. (2010, December 17). *A physicist solves the city.* Retrieved from http://www.nytimes.com/2010/12/19/magazine/19Urban_West-t.html?pagewanted=all&_r=0

Lim, W., & Plucker, J. A. (2001). Creativity through a lens of social responsibility: Implicit theories of creativity with Korean samples. *Journal of Creative Behavior, 35(2),* 115-130.

Lubart, T. I. (2010). Cross cultural perspectives on creativity. In J. C. Kaufman & R. J. Sternberg (Eds.) *The Cambridge handbook of creativity* (pp. 265-278). Cambridge, UK: Cambridge University Press.

Lubart T. I., & Georgsdottir, A. (2004). Creativity: Developmental and cross-cultural issues. In S. Lau, A. N. N. Hui, & G. Y. C. Ng (Eds.), *Creativity: When East meets West* (pp. 23-54). Danvers, MA: World Scientific Publishing.

Maslow, A. H. (1968). *Toward a psychology of being* (2nd ed.). Princeton, NJ: Van Nostrand.

Maslow, A. H. (1971). *The farther reaches of human nature.* New York, NY: Viking Press.

Mason, J. G. (1960). *How to be a more creative executive*. New York, NY: McGraw-Hill.

Maurat, S., Dernis, H., Webb, C., Spiezia, V., & Guellec, D. (2008). The OECD REGPAT database: A presentation. *OECD Science, Technology and Industry Working Papers, 2008/02*, OECD Publishing. doi:10.1787/241437144144

McLuhan, M., & Fiore, Q. (1968). *War and peace in the global village*. New York, NY: Bantam.

Mpofu, E., Myambo, K., Mogaji, A. A., Mashego, T-A., & Khaleefa, O. H. (2006). African perspectives on creativity. In J. C. Kaufman & R. J. Sternberg (Eds.), *The International handbook of creativity* (pp. 456-489). New York, NY: Cambridge University Press.

Murray, H. A. (1959). Vicissitudes of creativity. In H. H. Anderson (Ed.), *Creativity and its cultivation*. New York, NY: Harper & Row.

Ng, A. K., & Smith, I. (2004). Why is there a paradox in promoting creativity in the Asian classroom? In S. Lau, A. Hui, & G. Ng (Eds.), *Creativity: When East meets West* (pp. 87-112). Singapore: World Scientific.

Niu, W., & Kaufman, J. C. (2005). Creativity in troubled times: Factors associated with recognitions of Chinese literary creativity in the 20th century. *Journal of Creative Behavior, 39*(1), 57-67.

Niu, W., & Sternberg, R. J. (2002). Contemporary studies on the concept of creativity: The East and the West. *Journal of Creative Behavior, 36*(4), 269-288.

Niu, W., & Sternberg, R. J. (2003). Societal and school influence on students' creativity. *Psychology in the Schools, 40*(1),103-114.

Organisation for Economic Cooperation and Development (1994). *The measurement of scientific and technological advances: Using patent data as science and technology indicators patent manual*. Paris, France: OECD.

Puccio, G. & Grivas, C. (2009). Examining the relationship between personality traits and creativity styles. *Creativity and Innovation Management, 18*, 247–255.

Puccio, G. J., Mance, M., Switalski, L. B., & Reali, P. D. (2012). *Creativity rising: Creative thinking and creative problem solving in the 21st century*. Buffalo, NY: ICSC Press.

Pye, L. W. (2000). "Asian values": From dynamos to dominoes? In L. E. Harrison & S. P. Huntington (Eds.), *Culture matters: How values shape human progress* (pp. 244-255). New York, NY: Basic Books.

Radjou, N., Prabhu, J., Ahaju, S., & Roberts, K. (2012). *Jugaad innovation: Think frugal, be flexible, generate breakthrough growth*. San Francisco, CA: Jossey-Bass.

Raina, M. K. (1975). Parental perception about ideal child: A cross-cultural study. *Journal of Marriage and the Family, 37*(1), 229–232.

Raina, T. N., & Raina, M. K. (1971). Perception of teacher educators in India about the ideal pupil. *Journal of Educational Research, 64*(7), 303-306.

Rogers, C. (1961). *On becoming a person: A therapist's view of psychotherapy*. London, UK: Constable.

Rothwell, J. (2012, March 16). *Global innovation: The metropolitan edition*. Retrieved from http://www.newrepublic.com/blog/the-avenue/101780/global-innovation-the-metropolitan-edition

Rudowicz, E. (2003). Creativity and culture: A two-way interaction. *Scandinavian Journal of Educational Research, 47*(3), 273-290.

Runco, M. A. (2004). Personal creativity and culture. In S. Lau, A. N. N. Hui, & G. Y. C. Ng (Eds.), *Creativity: When East meets West* (pp. 9-21). Danvers, MA: World Scientific Publishing.

Runco, M. A., & Johnson, D. J. (2002). Parents' and teachers' implicit theories of children's creativity: A cross-cultural perspective. *Creativity Research Journal, 14*(3-4), 427-438.

Sachs, J. (2000). Notes on a new sociology of economic development. In L. E. Harrison & S. P. Huntington (Eds.), *Culture matters: How values shape human progress* (pp. 29-43). New York, NY: Basic Books.

Schomer, K. (2104, October 8). *Getting to Mars through Jugaad*. Retrieved from http://www.thehindu.com/opinion/op-ed/getting-to-mars-through-jugaad/article6479048.ece

Schumpeter, J. A. (1975). *Capitalism, socialism and democracy*. New York, NY: Harper.

Shostak, M. (1993). The creative individual in the world of the !Kung San. In S. Lavie, K. Narayan, & R. Rosaldo (Eds.), *Creativity/Anthropology* (pp. 54-69). Ithaca, NY: Cornell University Press.

Sternberg, R. J., Kaufman, J. C., & Pretz, J. E. (2002). *The creativity conundrum: A propulsion model of kinds of creative contributions*. East Sussex, UK: Psychology Press.

Sternberg, R. J., & Lubart, T. I. (1999). The concept of creativity: Prospects and paradigms. In R. J. Sternberg (Ed.), *Handbook of creativity*. Cambridge, UK: Cambridge University Press.

The Guardian (2010, November 17). *Press freedom: the Singapore grip*. Retrieved from http://www.theguardian.com/commentisfree/2010/nov/17/press-freedom-singapore-grip

Urabe, K., Child, J., & Kagono, T. (1988). *Innovation and management: International comparisons*. Berlin, NY: Walter de Gruyter.

von Franz, M.-L. (1995). *Creation myths*. Boston, MA: Shambhala Publications.

Ward, A. W. (1901). *A history of English dramatic literature to the death of Queen Anne*. London, England: Macmillan.

Weiner, R. P. (2000). *Creativity and beyond: Cultures, values and change*. Albany, NY: State University of New York Press.

Westwood, R., & Low, D. R. (2003). The multicultural muse: Culture, creativity and innovation. *International Journal of Cross Cultural Management*, 3(2), 235-259. doi:10.1177/14705958030032006

About the Author

Gaia Grant is the managing director of Tirian International Consultancy and the author of a number of books including *Who Killed Creativity?...And How Can We Get It Back?* (Jossey-Bass). Gaia has consulted for a wide range of organizations worldwide, from NGOs to Fortune500 companies, on building a culture that supports innovation.

Email: ggrant@tirian.com
Websites: www.tirian.com, www.whokilledcreativity.com
Twitter: @gaiagranttirian
Facebook: http://www.facebook.com/whokilledcreativity

Design Thinking: Is it the Only Approach We Need?

Courtney Zwart
International Center for Studies in Creativity
SUNY Buffalo State

Abstract

This paper explores whether alternative approaches to design thinking are needed in creative problem solving. It highlights the popularity of design thinking and explores why companies have adopted it. An overview of design thinking is provided, and its fundamentals and benefits are examined. Criteria for challenges appropriate for design thinking are reviewed, and conditions that support it are detailed. Finally, its limitations are discussed, and a potential way forward is identified.

Design Thinking: Is it the Only Approach We Need?

Currently the darling of problem solvers in both businesses and non-profits, *design thinking* is widely used to identify novel solutions to address organizational challenges and opportunities. Many Fortune 500 companies, including Procter & Gamble and Citrix, have sought to embed the methodology (Cohen, 2014; Martin, 2009). Some companies, such as Capital One, have gone so far as to establish a formal head of design thinking (Cohen, 2014). Using Google search results as a proxy for popularity (or at least available content), the search term "design thinking" (November 30, 2014) produced 1.3 million results, while the term "creative problem solving" produced 257,000.

Champions of design thinking are passionate about the approach's ability to address challenges large and small. Owen (2005) has even argued for the application of design thinking to decision making at the highest levels of policy to address problems caused by population growth, stress on resources, and the environment. Given its flexibility, robustness, and powerful results, one cannot help but wonder if design thinking obviates the need for any other problem solving approaches. This paper, then, explores the popularity, fundamentals, and benefits of design thinking, and offers a perspective on whether or not other approaches are needed.

Overview of an Approach

To understand its popularity, value and potential to eclipse other problem solving approaches, it is important to understand what design thinking is and where it comes from.

According to Bill Burnett (2013), executive director of the design program at Stanford University, design thinking's roots can be traced to 1963, the year that the board of trustees at Stanford University approved the establishment of a joint degree in art and engineering. A well-known graduate of the program, David Kelley, went on to found both the company that became IDEO and the Hasso Plattner Institute of Design at Stanford, also known as the d.school (Burnett, 2013).

Definitions of Design Thinking

As design thinking is an approach, and not a standardized and codified process, many different definitions of it exist. Cohen (2014) offered one of the most succinct, describing it as "a human-centered, prototype-driven process for innovation that can be applied to product, service, and business design" (p. 1). Razzouk and Shute (2012) termed it "an analytic and creative process that engages a person in opportunities to experiment, create and prototype models, gather feedback, and redesign" (p. 330).

Martin (2009) defined it as "thinking like a designer would" and indicated that "a person or organization instilled with that discipline is constantly seeking a fruitful balance between reliability and validity, between art and science, between intuition and analytics, and between exploration and exploitation" (p. 62). Martin (2009) also held that design thinking uses *abductive reasoning,* unlike approaches that use logical (and more-easily defensible) inductive and deductive reasoning. Abductive reasoning does not strive to prove that something is true or false; rather, its objective is to hypothesize what might be true. Abductive reasoning prioritizes new data, challenges assumptions, and seeks new possibilities.

Brown and Katz (2009) considered design thinking to be "a way of describing a set of principles that can be applied by diverse people to a wide range of problems" (p. 7) that span new physical products, processes, services, interactions, forms of entertainment, and ways of better working together. Instead of a linear series of steps, Brown and Katz (2009) envisioned design thinking as comprising three overlapping spaces: inspiration ("the problem or opportunity that motivates the search for solutions"), ideation ("the process of generating, developing and testing ideas") and implementation ("the path that leads from the project room to the market") (p. 16). Design thinking is iterative by nature, leaving one to adjust the approach as one's understanding of the problem evolves.

Liedtka and Ogilvie (2011) classified design thinking as a problem-solving approach that answers four key questions. These questions delineate stages of the specific design thinking approach that they advocate:

- *What is?* The current reality is explored and the problem, or opportunity is framed.

- *What if?* New possibilities for growth are generated.

- *What wows?* Assumptions are tested, and prototypes are created and refined.

- *What works?* Users are enrolled, and the solution is shaped into something that can be executed.

Fundamentals of Design Thinking

Design thinking derives power to produce truly novel solutions from several key principles. These principles also serve to distinguish the approach from other problem solving methodologies.

Human-centered and empathic. People and their fundamental unmet needs, stated or unstated, lie at the core of the design thinking process. Empathy, the ability to experience the world through the perspective of a potential user or customer, is key to identifying those needs. Tamara Christensen, an experienced design thinking practitioner, advised, "The capacity for deep feeling, for caring and for the desire to empathize with those around you is critical. It's important to embrace the messiness of human emotion and understand that people have complex inner lives" (personal communication, September 25, 2014).

Grounded in current state. The design thinking approach prioritizes a comprehensive understanding of the existing situation around a challenge or opportunity. A significant amount of time and other resources are expended up front to ensure this understanding. Tactics include both assessing existing data as well as gathering primary data, the latter through means such as ethnographic and observational research.

Focused on constraints. Constraints form the essential boundaries in which those applying design thinking must operate. The approach cannot function without constraints, which must ultimately be balanced in the solution for it to be successful. Brown and Katz (2009) defined three critical types of constraints:

> Constraints can best be visualized in terms of three overlapping criteria for successful ideas: feasibility (what is functionally possible within the foreseeable future); viability (what is likely to become part of a sustainable business model); and desirability (what makes sense to people and for people). (p. 18)

Insight-oriented. In design thinking, insights form the bridge between data gathered about a challenge or opportunity and generating concepts for potential solutions. Insights can be developed by identifying key themes in data gathered and then asking, "So what?" (Liedtka, 2014). The answer to that question becomes a platform from which to create ideas.

Optimistic. Liedtka (2014) characterized design thinking as guided by potential. Those successfully applying the approach truly believe they have the capacity to create solutions that address needs and improve situations. This requires confidence, which in turn requires trust (Brown & Katz, 2009).

Iterative. In design thinking, the path from an idea to a solution is not direct. Along the way, the idea may be reshaped, redirected and expanded, and then contracted. This is facilitated by prototyping, a key practice used throughout the process. Early in the process, prototypes are rudimentary. Later in the process, they become highly refined. Prototyping allows those applying the approach to "speak" the same language and provides learning that evolves the idea.

Focused on framing. Distinct and central to design thinking is the creation of frames, new ways from which to view problematic situations. A complex process, framing involves identifying a central paradox around the problem—that is, what makes the problem so hard to solve—searching the problem context for insights and clues, and observing the new frames that emerge (Dorst, 2011).

Dorst (2011) provided an example that helps to illustrate this process. A city was experiencing drunkenness, fights, theft, and drug dealing in its entertainment district. The local government responded by increasing police presence and hidden cameras, neither of which were effective in addressing the problem. Designers engaged to solve the problem determined that framing both the problem and solution as related to law and order was preventing the officials from identifying a solution. The designers conducted research to identify a new frame.

Through their research, the designers identified a few key themes: Those involved were young, non-criminals who wanted to have fun and became bored and frustrated over the course of a night out. The central conflict was that they were not, in fact, having a good time on their night out. The designers reframed the issue by studying the themes that emerged and identified an analogy with which to work: that of a large music festival. Reframing the entertainment district as that way enabled them to generate compelling ideas, such as providing later public transportation from the area and creating a smartphone app to tell those in clubs how long the line was at nearby clubs, obviating the street wandering that occurred when people found themselves faced with long lines at the new club.

Where It Works Best: Design Thinking at its Most Powerful

Liedtka and Ogilvie (2011) provided key criteria to determine a challenge's appropriateness for design thinking. The first criterion is whether or not the problem (or challenge) is human-centered—whether a deep understanding of the actual people (users) involved is possible and important. A second criterion is whether or not the problem (or challenge) is fully understood. In design thinking, defining the problem is as important as coming up with the solution. A third criterion relates to the level of certainty around the challenge or opportunity—i.e., a high level of uncertainty exists, and past data is unhelpful. A final criterion concerns the degree of complexity of the challenge or opportunity. Design thinking works best when the challenge is complex; e.g., when it is not easy to know where to start, and there are many connecting and interdependent facets of the problem.

How One Company Has Embraced Design Thinking

In 2000, A. G. Lafley, then the newly-appointed CEO of Proctor & Gamble (P&G), faced a critical business challenge: an unfavorable and declining ability to profitably create value for consumers (Martin, 2009). Successful new products were becoming scarce, while research and development costs were rising. Lafley understood that P&G had to simultaneously become more innovative and more efficient. He believed design thinking was the means by which to get there.

This meant turning P&G into a design organization. To do so, he created the company's first vice president for design strategy and innovation. He appointed Claudia Kotchka, an existing executive who had recently led a successful, internal innovation initiative, and gave her the mandate "to build P&G's design capability and act as the corporation's champion of design thinking" (Martin, 2009, p. 82). According to Martin, Kotchka accepted the challenge, and set out these steps:

- *Set expectations clearly up front and get your boss on board.* Kotchka created a contract with Lafley that outlined "what she could do, what she could not, and what she would need from him to make it happen" (p. 84). Kotchka attributed much of her ultimate success to this contract. Also key to her success was starting in a part of the company that was receptive to design thinking, instead of where she saw the greatest need.

- *Get help.* Kotchka realized that she needed senior design thinking experts, and, to do so, she enlisted the support of recruiters outside of the company.

- *Expect speed bumps.* Kotchka encountered challenges, including a corporate culture that was unsupportive of design thinking as well as suboptimal physical environments. A key act she took to address culture was to embed designers in the business units.

- *Don't try and talk—just demonstrate it.* To show to value of design thinking, Kotchka regularly sent senior executives out with designers "to experience firsthand how a designer observes, questions, and probes the hidden dimensions of the user experience" (p. 86).

Ultimately, Lafley and Kotchka's efforts to embed design thinking transformed P&G into a growth company and paid huge dividends. Within three years of Lafley's appointment as CEO, P&G's valuation had doubled and was delivering profit growth of 15% (Martin, 2009).

Problem-Solving Comparisons

Design thinking offers two distinct benefits over other problem-solving methodologies, such as Creative Problem Solving (CPS; Puccio, Mance, & Murdock, 2011): the focus on empathy, and prototyping. Given its user-centered nature, design thinking places a priority on empathizing with users. Critical to the approach is an in-depth understanding of not only what users say, but what they think, feel, and do related to the problem. CPS includes gathering key data around the problem, but it does not emphasize gaining a deep understanding of the user perspective.

CPS does not explicitly include prototyping (Puccio, Mance, & Murdock, 2011). Early in the process, prototypes are simple and rudimentary, but become increasingly refined toward the end of the process. Prototyping generates valuable feedback and learning from users, both of which serve to inform later prototypes. This subtracts risk from the design thinking solution.

One Option of Many

The benefits and advantages of design thinking are clear and widespread. However, upon examination, many of those same benefits and advantages also serve to limit the appropriateness of the approach and underscore the need for other problem solving strategies.

Not Every Challenge or Opportunity Is Human-Centered

Addressing unmet human needs does not lie at the core of all challenges facing businesses, organizations, and societies. Take, for example, challenges related to creating a new business model or problems associated with finding a new way to conduct molecular research. In other words, a consumer solution isn't always the end game.

Not Every Challenge Is Complex

Problems and challenges exist along a continuum of complexity. Applying a design thinking approach on one that lies towards the simpler end of the continuum, one without connecting and interdependent facets, is like using a sledgehammer when a ball-peen hammer will do. For these types of challenges, a less extensive and involved approach is more appropriate and efficient.

Design Thinking Is Not Standardized

Design thinking lacks both a standard definition and approach, and there is no consensus in the field on either. This lack of standardization makes it difficult to know which approach to select. And, even the most detailed approaches are difficult to follow for those who do not speak the language of design or who have not yet internalized a designer's mindset. Finally, what works in one area might not work in another. As Walters (2011) advised, "There's no plug-and-play system you can simply install and roll out" (p. 11).

Design Thinking Is Complex

A design thinking approach, done properly, unearths reams of primary and secondary data. After all these data are gathered comes the challenge of making sense of them—drawing insights and framing them to create platforms from which to ideate. This is time-consuming, difficult, and requires a team experienced in seeking patterns and distilling and synthesizing information.

Consensus Can Be Elusive

Design can be an alienating, even exclusive concept to many. Those from whom you need support and participation may be intimidated by a design thinking approach or consider it inappropriate for the task at hand. As Nussbaum (2011) stated, "In my experience, when you say the word 'design' to people across a table, they tend to smile politely and think 'fashion.' Say 'design thinking,' and they stop smiling and tend to lean away from you" (p. 1).

Design Thinking Is Challenging to Execute

Because it requires participation from a diverse set of individuals (often with contradictory viewpoints) and an organizational structure that supports cross-pollination of ideas, successful application of design thinking will likely require that an organization change its approach to innovation (Walters, 2011). In particular, the organizational structure as well as who is included in the process, will need to change. This can be a challenging for large, mature organizations that are resistant to changing systems and structures. In sum, implementing design thinking in an organization is an effort in change management (Liedtka, 2014).

Design Thinking Requires a Unique Leader and Team

Because it runs counter to how many organizations operate, successful design thinking efforts require leaders and participants who are committed, optimistic, and have a growth mindset. Hypothesizing about and prototyping against a future that does not exist (and, therefore, has no data to support it) is a challenge for many. Nussbaum (2011) concluded that operating independently of "'facts' provided by spreadsheets and data is anathema to most analysis-influenced C-suite members. But you need this kind of champion if design thinking is to gain traction and pay off" (p. 1). It is critical that the leader of the organization be someone who seeks validity over reliability.

Solutions Sometimes Lack Viability

While viability is a core constraint in some design thinking approaches, solutions reached often place a premium on consumer needs at the cost of financial feasibility. While the worlds of design and business are increasingly coming together, and business professionals have much to learn about design, so do design professionals have much to learn about ensuring a solution's financial viability. A chief innovation officer of a large bank that worked with a design thinking consultancy indicated "the business model was an afterthought" on his project (personal communication, February 12, 2014).

Conclusion

Design thinking is indeed a powerful approach, but it cannot be the only one. Because of differences in types of problems, organizations, organizational culture, leadership, time horizon, team composition, and resources, what is needed is an innovation toolkit consisting of a variety of problem solving processes.

Further, there is no need to adhere strictly to one approach. Problem-solving processes are flexible enough to allow for hybrid approaches. Having applied both design thinking and CPS, the author can readily see opportunities to enhance each approach with lessons from the other, such as by incorporating planning for action (creating implementation plans) into the former, and prototyping into the latter (Puccio, Mance, & Murdock, 2011).

Finally, challenges facing organizations and societies are growing in both number and complexity. To successfully address them, an improved understanding of the best approach, or elements of approaches, is needed to meet the challenge at hand. By collaborating with creativity practitioners, researchers should explore valid means by which this question can be answered, and optimal approaches can be determined.

References

Brown, T., & Katz, B. (2009). *Change by design: How design thinking transforms organizations and inspires innovation*. New York, NY: Harper Business.

Burnett, B. (2013, May 13). *Design thinking: Training yourself to be more creative* [video]. Retrieved from https://www.youtube.com/watch?v=34EuT2KH2Lw

Cohen, R. (2014, March 31). *Design thinking: A unified framework for innovation*. Retrieved from http://www.forbes.com/sites/reuvencohen/2014/03/31/design-thinking-a-unified-framework-for-innovation

Dorst, K. (2011). The core of "design thinking" and its application. *Design Studies*, 32(6), 521-532.

Liedtka, J. (2014). *Design thinking for innovative problem solving: A step-by-step project course* [Class lecture]. Retrieved from https://novoed.com

Liedtka, J., & Ogilvie, T. (2011). *Designing for growth: A design thinking tool kit for managers*. New York, NY: Columbia Business School Publishing.

Martin, R. L. (2009). *The design of business: Why design thinking is the next competitive advantage*. Cambridge, MA: Harvard Business Press.

Nussbaum, B. (2011, April 5). *Design thinking is a failed experiment. So what's next?* Retrieved from http://www.fastcodesign.com/1663558/design-thinking-is-a-failed-experiment-so-whats-next

Owen, C. (2005, October). *Design thinking. What it is. Why it is different. Where it has new value*. Speech presented at the International Conference on Design Research and Education for the Future, Gwangju City, Korea.

Puccio, G. J., Mance, M., & Murdock, M. C. (2011). *Creative leadership: Skills that drive change* (2nd ed.). Thousand Oaks, CA: Sage.

Razzouk, R., & Shute, V. (2012). What is design thinking and why is it important? *Review of Educational Research*, 82(4), 330-348.

Walters, H. (2011, March 24). *"Design thinking" isn't a miracle cure, but here's how it helps*. Retrieved from http://www.fastcodesign.com/1663480/design-thinking-isnt-a-miracle-cure-but-heres-how-it-helps

About the Author

Courtney Zwart is an innovation expert with extensive experience creating and implementing novel solutions to business challenges. She consults for Fortune 500 companies, and instructs on creativity in the State University of New York system and at the Creative Problem Solving Institute. She holds an MBA, and a Master of Science degree in Creativity from the International Center for Studies in Creativity at SUNY Buffalo State.

Email: courtneyzwart@gmail.com
Website: www.courtneyzwart.branded.me
Twitter: @courtney_zwart
LinkedIn: https://www.linkedin.com/in/courtneyzwart

Acknowledgments

Paul Reali at ICSC Press has been a standard bearer for the *Big Questions in Creativity* series since its inception, and he is a steady source of focus and conviction. With this third edition, our gratitude for his talents has grown exponentially. The same can be said for Kevin Opp's handsome design, also a constant since the start.

We owe our colleagues special thanks. At the International Center for Studies in Creativity at SUNY Buffalo State, the abiding support of Gerard Puccio, Creative Studies department chair, and Rita Zientek, associate dean of the School of the Professions, has been invaluable. Selcuk Acar, John Cabra, Roger Firestien, Jon Michael Fox, Sue Keller-Mathers, and Jo Yudess sharpen the questions all creativity scholars must ask. David Gauntlett at the University of Westminster has been generous with his support and exceptional editorial clarity. Julia Figliotti, an ICSC alumna and contributor to the 2014 edition, has been more than a capable proofreader—she is a master of style and creativity, too. Marie Mance, accomplished author and expert on the nuances of editing, has brought her prowess to this series since its inception and has our lasting gratitude.

For their continuous resilience, insight, and not entirely un-coincidental prowess in Creative Problem Solving, we are especially grateful to Cullen Clark of the University of Alabama-Birmingham and Andy Burnett of Knowinnovation Ltd.

Finally, our deepest appreciation goes to the contributors to *Big Questions in Creativity 2015*. Their work reflects the kaleidoscopic nature of the field, and hints at a colorful future.

About the Editors

Mary Kay Culpepper is a doctoral researcher and visiting lecturer in the faculty of Media, Arts and Design at the University of Westminster in London. Her work focuses on the individual, social, and cultural barriers and affordances to creativity. Ms. Culpepper holds an M.Sc. in Creative Studies from SUNY Buffalo State, where she was named a Mary C. Murdock scholar in 2011, and a B.A. in Journalism from the University of Mississippi. Before resuming her studies, Ms. Culpepper was a nationally recognized newspaper and magazine journalist, and was editor-in-chief of *Cooking Light* magazine, the largest-circulation epicurean magazine in the country during her tenure.

Email: marykayculpepper@gmail.com
Twitter: @marykculpepper
Web: MaryKayCulpepper.com

Dr. Cyndi Burnett is an Assistant Professor at the International Center for Studies in Creativity at Buffalo State. She implements the Center's efforts to "ignite creativity around the world," and her work includes projects such as: developing online 3D creativity labs, connecting communities of creative thinkers via social media, and designing a Massive Open Online Course (MOOC) on Everyday Creativity.

Prior to becoming an academic, Dr. Burnett was a professional actress. Having performed in many stage productions, she realized that she had developed a passionate interest in the underlying processes involved in creation. This realization led to her studying creativity at the ICSC and ultimately gaining her Ed.D. in Curriculum, Teaching and Learning from the University of Toronto.

Her research interests include: understanding creativity in a hyper-connected world, holistic approaches to Creative Problem Solving, creative thinking in higher education, and the use of creative models and techniques in children. She was recently featured in an article in the *New York Times* titled, "Creativity Becomes an Academic Discipline."

Twitter: @CyndiBurnett
Facebook: https://www.facebook.com/cyndiaburnett
Email: argonac@buffalostate.edu

The International Center for Studies in Creativity

Creativity, creative problem solving, and change leadership play a major role in today's workplace. Professional success is linked to the ability to master creativity, to operate as a creative problem solver, to innovate and to lead change. The need for people to cope with and direct change in their lives and in their organizations has become increasingly apparent. At the International Center for Studies in Creativity (ICSC), we strive to develop and nurture critical life skills in our students. The approaches we teach are applied successfully to educational, business, and industrial settings. Our graduates report that the skills and lessons learned at the ICSC have had a profound impact on their lives and organizations.

The ICSC is recognized for offering "The Credential in Creativity" for more than 40 years, a Master of Science degree and a graduate certificate in Creativity and Change Leadership. These programs are designed to provide professionals with the necessary skills to become transformational leaders in their organizations and communities. With our international reputation, we attract students from around the world. The Master of Science and graduate certificate are available on campus, as well as to distance learners.

The ICSC is a unique academic unit within SUNY Buffalo State. Since 1967, we have trained students, groups, teams and organizations to become more effective creative thinkers and problem solvers and to instill these skills in others. As the first school to offer a Master of Science degree in creativity, the ICSC has achieved an international reputation for scholarly research and teaching that focuses on developing creativity, leadership, decision-making and problem-solving skills. We invite you to explore the many opportunities that are available through our educational programs. Please visit creativity.buffalostate.edu.

ICSC Press

Created in 2012, ICSC Press is the imprint of the International Center for Studies in Creativity. The mission of the press supports the vision of the Center to ignite creativity around the world, facilitating the recognition of creative thinking as an essential life skill.

ICSC Press's goal is to put the work of our best teachers, thinkers, and practitioners into the hands of a wide audience, making titles available quickly and in multiple formats, both paper and electronic.

To learn more, to purchase titles, or to submit a proposal, visit icscpress.com.

More than 5000 readers in six countries!

CREATIVITYRISING

Creative Thinking and Creative Problem Solving in the 21st Century

Gerard J. Puccio, Marie Mance, Laura Barbero Switalski, Paul D. Reali

Living Creatively in the 21st Century

The need for creativity has never been greater. In fact, we chose the title, *Creativity Rising: Creative Thinking and Creative Problem Solving in the 21st Century,* to reflect this belief. If we are to live healthy, productive lives in this century we must develop the mind-set and the skill set for effectively responding to and initiating change. *Creativity Rising* is both a why-to and how-to guide to help you create your own future.

In this book we:

- explore the nature of creativity

- debunk common myths about creativity

- describe the rapid rise of change in the 21st century

- outline the Creative Problem Solving process, an approach to on-demand creativity

ICSC PRESS
INTERNATIONAL CENTER *for* STUDIES *in* CREATIVITY
BUFFALO STATE · The State University of New York

icscpress.com/creativityrising | creativity.buffalostate.edu | Twitter hashtag #creativityrising

Big Questions in Creativity 2014:
A Collection of First Works, Vol. 2

Edited by Mary Kay Culpepper & Cynthia Burnett

What is creativity? Can it be taught? How is it measured? What are the stakes for neglecting it? And what opportunities beckon for the people and organizations who dare to embrace it? At the International Center for Studies in Creativity at SUNY Buffalo State, home of the world's first Master of Science degree in Creativity, scholars seek those answers every day. And in *Big Questions in Creativity 2014*, the field's newest thinkers tackle some of its most intriguing questions. As students and recent graduates of the program, they represent a variety of cultures, experiences, and backgrounds. Yet they are united in their energetic exploration of current issues in creativity and their passion for knowing more.

Society and Creativity

- Eva Teruzzi: Product measurement: How do I know it is creative?
- Julia Figliotti: What is the correlation between mental health and creativity?
- Rumman Ahmad: Does culture affect creativity and innovation? An emic perspective from Pakistan
- Adela Vangelisti: What are the relationships between creativity and the choreographic process?

Organizational Creativity

- José Pablo Alcázar Zamacona: Should creativity be a strategic tool for 21st century organizations?
- Linda Salna: Why is creative thinking important now?

Individual Creativity

- Mariano Tosso: How to unlock the potential of your insight?
- Darlene Kent: Fail UP: How might we embrace failure?

Education & Creativity

- Dee Langsenkamp: How might creativity enhance the future of gifted and talented education?

ICSC Press
International Center *for* Studies *in* Creativity
Buffalo State · The State University of New York

icscpress.com/bigquestions | creativity.buffalostate.edu

Lightning Source UK Ltd.
Milton Keynes UK
UKOW04f1837191115

263110UK00001B/158/P